Think It. Be It. Live It.
90 Days of Inspiration

Think It. Be It. Live It.
90 Days of Inspiration

Alexander L. Brown

ABrown Enterprises

Printed in the United States of America

First Printing, 2020

ISBN 9-7817352-575-01 (Paperback)
ISBN 9-7817352575-18 (ePub)

ABrown Enterprises
PO Box 1381
Stockbridge, GA 30281

DEDICATION

This book is dedicated to my amazing wife Leah. Without you none of this is possible. Secondly, this is for my 3 children Amayah, Alex, and Ariel who are a constant reminder of authentic love. I still can't believe God allows me to be your father. Lastly, I'd like to dedicate this book to every person who will read and make the decision to think it, be it, and live it.

Table of Contents

WELCOME TO GO

There is a greater you inside of you. "Wait!! Say what?" is probably what you're thinking. As you read this book, you may very well experience several thoughts. I challenge you not to stop but to continue to go forward, even when it seems tough. The greater you, inside of you, is just waiting to emerge, so expect to overcome some obstacles. In the end, you will be so much better because of it. Your eyes are reading a book that was designed to support your growth toward identifying and fulfilling your purpose, while also starting the process of building a lasting legacy. You are not alone. Let's go on this journey together.

There's no looking back, so let's get started.

THINK IT

Day 1: IN THE BEGINNING

As young children, we all had dreams of becoming something great when we grew up. We had great dreams, and the word *can't* was not a part of our vocabulary. Somewhere along the path, many dreams may have gone away, or we conformed to the expectations of others.

Many of us have high expectations for the year. It is important to not conform to the limitations that are imposed on us by other people. The enemy wants to discourage you and break your spirit because you have great potential. In the beginning months, you need a few victories under your belt because that builds your confidence and drives your ambition.

The hardest part about achieving your goals is the beginning. Push past the initial barriers and take those first steps. For example, you may initially feel like you are tired, but once you get to the gym to work out, you begin to feel a lot better. In the beginning: 1) Do not conform, 2) Set your mind on high expectations, and 3) Push past those obstacles in your path. Your victory is just on the other side of the door.

THINK IT

Reflection

_____
_____
_____
_____
_____
_____
_____
_____
_____
_____
_____
_____
_____
_____

Action

_____
_____
_____
_____
_____
_____
_____
_____
_____
_____
_____
_____
_____
_____
_____

Day 2: BORN TO WIN

When you look back over your life, what do you feel that you were born to do? I certainly understand that various people throughout your life may have made comments about what they think you should do with your life. However, you must make the ultimate decision as to how you wish to live your life.

You were not born to just walk the Earth for fifty, sixty, or seventy years or to just take up space. Your current situations do not define your future because we live in a world that is always changing. Only you have the power and authority to claim that you were born to win. Everyone has to live life, so why not live life to its fullest potential? However, in order to live life to the fullest, you must first realize that life is not always going to be easy, but you were still born to win.

Before you entered your mother's womb, you were carefully crafted. You were designed with specialized tools. You may not be living to your full potential because you are trying to do and accomplish what everyone around you is doing. However, you will never live up to your potential trying to mimic someone else's actions. If you would just take a deeper look at what God has given you, you would realize that you were born to win. Regardless of your childhood and upbringing, it is still possible to succeed. Your birth was a special occasion, and on the day of you birth, you were given a purpose. It is time to open the gifts that you were given.

Reflection

_____
_____
_____
_____
_____
_____
_____
_____
_____
_____
_____
_____
_____
_____
_____

Action

_____
_____
_____
_____
_____
_____
_____
_____
_____
_____
_____
_____
_____
_____
_____

Day 3: SET APART

Have you taken the time to think about why you were made the way that you were? If you look at the people around you, you will find that they also have two eyes, one nose, and a mouth, just like you do, but you look completely different because God took the time to design every detail of your physical makeup and internal structure.

If you have been wondering why it has been so difficult to fit in with certain crowds or be in certain relationships, it may be because you have been set apart. You are trying to force yourself to fit into a space that is not meant for you to occupy. For example, a car may only seat five people, but if you attempt to force two or three other people in it, I can assure you that it will be an uncomfortable ride. There is a reason why you do not fit in with some people. Your life has been stamped by God with a seal of distinction, and He has set you apart to lift you up. A separation has taken place, and it has been done in your favor.

Yes, you are different, and you should be excitedly anticipating what is awaiting you in your future. You do not have to think, act, and speak as the so-called in-crowd does, so do not allow anyone to pressure you to fit in where you were not meant to be in the first place. Set the standard and be true to yourself. Your life should not be led by the expectations of others. Do not conform just so you can be a part of something that, in the long run, is not in your best interest. You may have to stand firm and stand alone, but God will bring you like-minded people in preparation for your future. You are set apart.

THINK IT

Reflection

_____
_____
_____
_____
_____
_____
_____
_____
_____
_____
_____
_____
_____
_____
_____
_____

Action

_____
_____
_____
_____
_____
_____
_____
_____
_____
_____
_____
_____
_____
_____
_____

Day 4: MOVING PAST BAD DECISIONS

If you are reading this message, you have survived. You may not be where you want to be yet, but you have lived to see another day. Making a bad decision does not mean you have to stay in that state of mind. Remember, you are human. You are not perfect. Do not let someone degrade you or bring you down because of a bad decision. That bad decision does not define who you are, and God is working it out on your behalf. Pick your head up, walk with confidence, and learn from your mistake. Today is a new day filled with new opportunities, so do not let the disappointments of yesterday hinder your future.

THINK IT

Reflection

_____
_____
_____
_____
_____
_____
_____
_____
_____
_____
_____
_____
_____
_____
_____
_____

Action

_____
_____
_____
_____
_____
_____
_____
_____
_____
_____
_____
_____
_____
_____
_____
_____

Day 5: SO?

Many of us have signature words or phrases that we like to use when having discussions. We use certain words so often that other people can tell who said it without us being physically present. Here is another word that you can add to your arsenal: "So."

Many times people are just not known by the good they have done or the success they have in their lives but rather by their mistakes and failures. It may seem that, no matter how many times you do things right, one wrong action will always stand out. Do not allow anyone to throw your mistakes in your face when you are working hard to make your dreams come true. Yeah, you made a mistake or a wrong decision, but tell that person "so." We are all inadequate and imperfect people, so when we make mistakes, we should have people who are willing to encourage and build us up and not tear us down.

Has anyone ever told you that you are not who they thought you were? Well, they may be right. They may have known you back then, but you have a right to grow up and change. If you are honestly making strides in a positive direction and they thought you were a different type of person, that is not your problem. You do not have to change who you are to fit the kind of person someone else thought you should be. A few may stop hanging around you — so. Some may call you names — so. Many may turn their backs on you — so.

Some people lack self-esteem because they are allowing the words of others to dictate their mindset. That may have worked last year, but things are going to change this year. Remember the word "so."

THINK IT

Reflection

_____
_____
_____
_____
_____
_____
_____
_____
_____
_____
_____
_____
_____
_____
_____

Action

_____
_____
_____
_____
_____
_____
_____
_____
_____
_____
_____
_____
_____
_____
_____

Day 6: CONSCIOUS DECISIONS

One of the worst decisions you can ever make is to not make a decision at all. If you fail to make a decision, life will push you around, and you will find yourself subjected to the roller coaster of life. You'll be unsure of the speed changes and let downs, and you'll be jerked through the things you cannot control. No one is better informed or equipped to make an accurate decision about the path of your life than the person you see looking back at you in the mirror. Does it make sense to allow someone from the outside looking in to dictate how you should live your life?

Regardless of who you are, you only have one life to live, and life is too precious to allow someone else to live it for you. Decide today that you will not live your life through the perspective of someone else's eyes. At the end of the day, no one cares more about you and your future than you. While some may have your best interest at heart, you still need to be the CEO of your actions. It is not a good decision to put your life in the hands of another individual because that person has his or her own insecurities, idiosyncrasies, and imperfections. By attempting to please everyone, you will satisfy no one. Your energy will be drained. Your time will be lost, and unneeded stress will be added to your life. Release the weight of last year and decide that this is truly a year of opportunity.

THINK IT

Reflection

_____
_____
_____
_____
_____
_____
_____
_____
_____
_____
_____
_____
_____
_____

Action

_____
_____
_____
_____
_____
_____
_____
_____
_____
_____
_____
_____
_____

Day 7: QUICK REACTIONS

One of the problems that many of us have is reacting too quickly and without giving our decisions proper thought. It is difficult to make a sound decision when you allow your emotions to think for you. We have to be careful with our emotions because quick reactions can cause costly damage. No relationship will be perfect at all times. There will be difficult times. Before you react, allow yourself to step away from the situation and think. If you do not have peace in your mind, you may be surprised at what comes out of your mouth. We must place a guard on our mouths.

As children, we heard the saying, "Sticks and stones may break my bones, but words will never hurt me." I have to disagree. If you hear harmful words from someone that you love and cherish, they will hurt. While it can be difficult, in order to sustain relationships, it is critically necessary to take the time to stop and think before speaking too quickly. It may take time, but you must be aware of what the enemy tries to place in your mind because eventually it will come out of your mouth.

Today, take a moment to think before you respond.

THINK IT

Reflection

_____
_____
_____
_____
_____
_____
_____
_____
_____
_____
_____
_____
_____
_____

Action

_____
_____
_____
_____
_____
_____
_____
_____
_____
_____
_____
_____
_____

Day 8: THE ROOT OF THE PROBLEM

It does not matter who you are, where you come from, or what you say, everyone has an unfavorable perception about some area of their lives. Some people are disappointed by what they see in the mirror. Some feel broken because of a lack of finances, and there are countless other situations that can be burdensome.

What are you hiding from the world? How long are you going to allow one problem area to defeat you? Only you know what lies on the inside of your mind, and until you decide to honestly face the issue, you will not overcome the situation. Your dreams need support, and it is crucially necessary that you abandon negative thoughts. You are not stuck, and you are not required to accept defeat. The healing and rebuilding process can begin today if you openly express your heartfelt desires to God and make the effort to strive for victory. Stop dealing with your areas of hurt merely at the surface level and dig deeper to the root of the issue.

Some of us have been dealing with the same problem for too long, and the chain of bad days must now be broken. It is time to rise to a higher level. As you do this, it may be necessary to leave some things from your past behind. You might need to separate yourself from negative people in order to make a positive change. Do not be afraid of change because enough is enough. It may be a long process, but the first steps must be taken now.

THINK IT

Reflection

_____
_____
_____
_____
_____
_____
_____
_____
_____
_____
_____
_____
_____

Action

_____
_____
_____
_____
_____
_____
_____
_____
_____
_____
_____
_____
_____
_____

Day 9: RESTORATION

Have you been restored from what you previously endured? As we go through the year, we deal with numerous energy-draining activities. Unfortunately, we can, sometimes, become so involved in work, relationships, and more work that we fail to rest. If you maintain this type of daily routine for extended periods of time, you will find yourself living an unbalanced lifestyle.

Some of us have been telling ourselves that we need some rest and more personal time, but each day seems to take more and more. If you have found yourself in this position, you need some restoration. Grass fades and leaves dry up if they have received too much sun and an insufficient amount of water and nutrients. Likewise, you also need to be replenished. If you do not know when to say when, life will continue to take your time without asking permission.

Throughout the year, we face battles and must deal with life's ups and downs. While this is occurring, you may lose some of the essential tools that are needed to lead a fulfilling life. Those tools are: 1) clarity of vision, 2) a growing understanding of purpose, 3) persistence, and 4) the ability to evaluate and adjust. God will not only restore and refill what you've already lost; He will also abundantly bless you with more than you could have ever imagined.

THINK IT

Reflection

_____
_____
_____
_____
_____
_____
_____
_____
_____
_____
_____
_____
_____
_____
_____

Action

_____
_____
_____
_____
_____
_____
_____
_____
_____
_____
_____
_____
_____
_____

Day 10: UP AGAINST THE WALL

What happens when certain situations or circumstances continuously push you into an uncomfortable position? Rather than stepping forward, do you keep backing up? Some obstacles may seem too big to overcome, so you back up because you are operating in fear. In other situations, you just may not know how to face what is in front of you. Well, you can only back up so far, and you will (if you have not already) eventually find yourself with your back up against the wall. The initial reaction to this position may make you nervous, but it is actually a blessing in disguise. When you find yourself with your back up against the wall, you are in the best fighting position. There is nowhere else to go but forward, so you must face whatever obstacle is blocking your path. This position brings out the best in you. Prior to this type of situation, you may not have known what strengths you possessed. You may not have known what was lying dormant inside you. Desperate situations draw an inner fortitude out of you because you are in survival mode. It is time to stop backing up. It is time to press forward. The problem may seem big, but it is no match for God. It is necessary to have faith and believe. When you can no longer step backward, you have no choice but to press forward.

THINK IT

Reflection

_____
_____
_____
_____
_____
_____
_____
_____
_____
_____
_____
_____
_____
_____
_____

Action

_____
_____
_____
_____
_____
_____
_____
_____
_____
_____
_____
_____
_____
_____

Day 11: INADEQUATE

Many of us must face circumstances that seem too big at first glance. After looking at the situation, you may find yourself questioning your abilities and strengths. Sometimes we can visualize what we desire to achieve, but the road ahead may appear to be intimidating or too rough to handle. Well, you are not inadequate. You may look in the mirror every day and still not realize what you truly possess on the inside. If you look back over your life, you will realize that you have not gotten where you are today without facing some struggles, without enduring some difficult times. Stumbling blocks may have tripped you up. Friends may have let you down, and some relationships may have been broken, but you made it through. Many of us need to change the way we perceive ourselves. If you are already thinking you cannot win, then you are starting off at a disadvantage because you have a defeatist mentality. You must first believe in what you already possess. Reach deep down within yourself and recognize that you were not born to fail.

Continue to strengthen your mentality and attitude; remember that there is more in you than you think.

Reflection

_____

_____

_____

_____

_____

_____

_____

_____

_____

_____

_____

_____

_____

_____

Action

_____

_____

_____

_____

_____

_____

_____

_____

_____

_____

_____

_____

_____

_____

Day 12: WHO DO YOU THINK YOU ARE?

When you look in the mirror, what is the first thing you see? Do you see a confident, intelligent, and unique creation filled with extraordinary potential, or do you see a weak, dumb, and ordinary person who will never amount to anything? If you see the latter of the two, YOU ARE WRONG!

If no one else tells you for the rest of the year, I'm going to tell you something right now. God does not create junk, and if you are breathing, there is still hope for your future. You do not have to accept the discouraging words of parents or peers who have spoken negative words into your life. Today, you must begin to acknowledge that you are a beautiful creature with extraordinary potential. There is no one else like you on the face of this earth.

When you were created, every detail of your physical makeup was carefully crafted. Your personality and inner qualities were by no means a mistake. The world needs you, just the way you are, to make a significant impact. I encourage you not to look down when you walk today because you need the world to see the face that is destined for success.

Reflection

_____
_____
_____
_____
_____
_____
_____
_____
_____
_____
_____
_____
_____

Action

_____
_____
_____
_____
_____
_____
_____
_____
_____
_____
_____
_____
_____
_____

Day 13: THE INSIDE TRULY COUNTS

Can you judge a book by its cover? Many of us make quick decisions about what we see every day. At the same time, many people look at you and make decisions based on what they see. Is that fair? If you spend time worrying about what everybody else thinks, you will stop focusing on what God has called you to be. If you make mistakes, people are going to talk about you, and if you succeed, people are definitely going to talk about you. What we must learn to do is thank God for the ups and downs and seek His will for our lives.

No matter who you are and what you do for people, not everyone is going to like you. If they judge you before they get to know the real you, then that is their fault, and they are probably missing out on a great friend. That is not your problem. Continue to be faithful to yourself and do not degrade yourself by lowering your standards to satisfy someone else's temporary needs.

THINK IT

Reflection

_____
_____
_____
_____
_____
_____
_____
_____
_____
_____
_____
_____
_____
_____
_____

Action

_____
_____
_____
_____
_____
_____
_____
_____
_____
_____
_____
_____
_____
_____

Day 14: WHO DEFINES YOU?

Are you confident in who you are? Why is it that so many of us take so much time and energy out of the day to prove to other people who we are on the inside? We want to impress people, so they will approve of us. At the end of the day, the only things that really matter are that: 1) You please God, and 2) You are happy with what you see in the mirror.

Unfortunately, other people often see greater qualities in you than you see in yourself. Therefore, they will try to limit you and cause you to stay at their level because they do not want you to succeed. Envy, unhappiness, and jealousy like your company. Do not let anyone put you into his or her box of thinking and define you by how he or she thinks you ought to be. The world around you will think differently about you every day, so do not waste your valuable time trying to prove to someone else what God has already designed into your character. Since we all have flaws, we should be using our strengths to make an even greater impact. Think big, take the first step, and enjoy the journey ahead.

THINK IT

Reflection

_____
_____
_____
_____
_____
_____
_____
_____
_____
_____
_____
_____
_____
_____
_____
_____

Action

_____
_____
_____
_____
_____
_____
_____
_____
_____
_____
_____
_____
_____
_____
_____

Day 15: DO YOU HAVE TIME?

It is important that we take advantage of our time. Oftentimes, when you are in a particular age group, you may feel that you are invincible and have plenty of time left in your life. In some cases, such as with investing, time may be on your side. However, what we often fail to take seriously is that decisions made at an early age have long-term impacts.

I have heard too many stories about how an older and wiser individual wished he or she could go back and do it all over again. I encourage you to decide to not put yourself in the same position. A key to using your time to your advantage is to FOCUS. Time can be your greatest asset and tool if it is used wisely. Shake your family tree and set a new direction for future generations by maximizing your time. Regardless of where you started, God is more interested in where you end up. Your tomorrow is affected by your today. Take a few minutes out of your busy schedule to take care of yourself.

Do not get so caught up with school, work, and your daily routine that you do not recognize what is most important. Plant the seed now, give it TIME, and later, you will enjoy the sweetest fruits from your hard work.

THINK IT

Reflection

_____
_____
_____
_____
_____
_____
_____
_____
_____
_____
_____
_____
_____
_____

Action

_____
_____
_____
_____
_____
_____
_____
_____
_____
_____
_____
_____
_____
_____

Day 16: NEXT-LEVEL THINKING

What level are you operating on right now? If you are playing the game on the same level that you did one, two, or three years ago, then it is time for an increase. Some of us know what we should be doing, but we are afraid to move and leave our comfort zone. The other side of it is that some of us know what we should be doing, but we are afraid we will fail. Fear is one of the greatest hindrances of your rise to the next level.

While you may be busy being afraid of what you may not accomplish, your enemies are afraid of what you will accomplish. The enemy plants some stumbling blocks in your mind because he knows that, if he can capture your mind, he can control your actions and destroy your progress. This year, it is time to go to a new level. Some of the things that bothered you last year have to be left in last year. If you are determined and passionate about a subject, then you must begin to walk in your victory. When you begin to have a next-level mentality, many of the small things will not bother you anymore. Honestly, some things just do not deserve your attention, and you must release unnecessary weight in order to soar to a new level. Next-level thinking requires you to release that extra weight so that you can go to higher heights. Be mindful of the activities in your life that absorb your time beyond the necessary requirement.

Your journey toward next-level thinking begins today.

THINK IT

Reflection

_____
_____
_____
_____
_____
_____
_____
_____
_____
_____
_____
_____
_____
_____
_____
_____

Action

_____
_____
_____
_____
_____
_____
_____
_____
_____
_____
_____
_____
_____
_____
_____
_____

Day 17: FINDING YOUR WAY IN THE DARK

How many times have you walked into a dark room with your hands out, reaching to find the light switch? You may have stumbled over a few things, banged your foot against something, and broken a couple of items along the way. If you have never experienced this, take the time to blindfold yourself and try to walk around your house with no help.

In actuality, this is exactly what many of us do every day. If you are not working toward a defined purpose and a desired goal, then you are aimlessly wandering around every morning when you open your eyes. Without a blueprint of what you want to fulfill in your life, time is just passing you by. I know you have heard an older individual say, "I wish I would have started when I was younger." Well, you have the opportunity to start right now. All of us have some dark areas in our lives, but that doesn't mean we have to remain in darkness.

You turn on the light in your life by working to fulfill what God has already predestined for your life. No matter who or where you are, we are all a "work in progress." We are all incomplete, and we need to build strong foundations in order to have generational success. The deeper the roots of the tree, the taller the tree can grow and, eventually, bear fruit. The same goes for you and me. Begin to plant good seeds in your own life, and years from now, you will reap the harvest of what you have sown for many years. If these words have not pushed you to take action, take the time to ask those who are older than you what they wish they had accomplished in their younger years.

THINK IT

Reflection

_____
_____
_____
_____
_____
_____
_____
_____
_____
_____
_____
_____
_____
_____

Action

_____
_____
_____
_____
_____
_____
_____
_____
_____
_____
_____
_____
_____
_____

Day 18: A BLURRED VISION

What happens when you are not able to clearly see how you are supposed to get to your desired goals? It may seem that life is taking you in a different direction that is the opposite of your original plans.

How many times have you been trying to read something that is far away or see something on the television, but it was hard for you to see? What did you do? More than likely, you squinted your eyes so that you could FOCUS, and slowly but surely, you began to see what you wanted to read.

When your vision seems blurry, it is time to focus. One of the worst things that you can do when you are not sure what direction to move in is to act out of frustration. That will only further complicate your situation. You must stand firm and strong and ask God to give you direction. The weather forecast for your life is not always going to be "clear skies with a temperature of 76 degrees and no signs of thunderstorms." When every other thing seems that it is falling apart, you must hold on to the vision that has been placed in your heart. You can be a top businessperson, an accountant, a doctor, an architect, or whatever your heart desires. Ask God to place a fortress around your vision and protect you from harm. When others seek to destroy your vision because they are not able to see what you are trying to accomplish, then you must step away. It is not their vision because God gave it to you.

THINK IT

Reflection

_____

_____

_____

_____

_____

_____

_____

_____

_____

_____

_____

_____

_____

_____

Action

_____

_____

_____

_____

_____

_____

_____

_____

_____

_____

_____

_____

_____

_____

Day 19: TUNNEL VISION

When you think about what your life will look like five, ten, or twenty years from now, what comes to mind? Do you feel that you are limited to a certain lifestyle because you came from a certain background? If so, you are thinking entirely too small. Your tunnel vision has locked your mind into a specific idea and has placed boundaries on how far you can go.

We must learn to think bigger than anyone else in our families. Pave a new way of thinking for your family to follow, so they will also be released from limiting, traditional thoughts. It is crucially important to write the vision down and be clear about what you desire to accomplish. You may be asking yourself, "What if I fall short of these big dreams?" Well, if you shoot for your biggest dream and fall short, you will still be ten times ahead of how far you originally thought you could go.

THINK IT

Reflection

_____
_____
_____
_____
_____
_____
_____
_____
_____
_____
_____
_____
_____
_____

Action

_____
_____
_____
_____
_____
_____
_____
_____
_____
_____
_____
_____
_____
_____

Day 20: THE BATTLE WITHIN

The most difficult battles you will face are often not external quarrels but internal struggles. We walk past people every day, and while the outside appearance seems okay, that individual may be dealing with a tug-of-war in their minds. There are feelings of depression, thoughts of suicide, questioning "am I good enough?", imposter syndrome. The list goes on with various extremes. Unfortunately, no one is exempt from these battles, and the key is to not remain isolated. The key to lessening the blows of this battle often happens through community.

I certainly understand that you must be careful with whom you share private information, but it is critical to build trusting relationships. Oftentimes, when we are dealing with life's greatest battles, we are not able to contact the people we need to communicate with during our time of need. That person may not answer the phone. He or she may be at work, or the person may not be at home. You are seeking answers to your problems, or you may just be looking for someone to listen to. And while cell phones are extremely popular, sometimes other people's lines are busy, so you may be out of your network service area, or your call may be dropped. Then, what do you do?

When everything else fails, remember that the line of communication, through prayer, is always open to God. The signal always has full bars. You have access to the largest network provider. It has a track record of no dropped calls, and you have unlimited minutes and data. Rest in the truth that He desires to hear from you.

Reflection

_____

_____

_____

_____

_____

_____

_____

_____

_____

_____

_____

_____

_____

_____

_____

_____

Action

_____

_____

_____

_____

_____

_____

_____

_____

_____

_____

_____

_____

_____

_____

_____

Day 21: YOU DO NOT LIVE HERE

Why won't they just go home? How many times have you had people overstay their welcome at your house, especially when it was getting late and you were ready for them to go home? You yawned visibly and acted like you were getting sleepy to show them that it was time to go, but they just did not get the point. Hopefully, you did not have to force them to get out.

We all go through different periods of lack. At times, you may not have enough money, or you may be depressed, and things are just not going your way. In life, we all must go through these dry periods, but it is not a permanent situation. A good mentor taught me that "broke is temporary, but poor is permanent." Do not allow negative people to get into your mind and tell you that you are poor. I am not solely referring to money, but poor in your mind, spirit, and physical make up as well. It is time to kick those thoughts out the door because they have overstayed their visit. Mediocrity has no place in place in your life. Lack cannot stay in the guest bedroom. Poverty cannot ring your doorbell, and broke is banned from your living room.

THINK IT

Reflection

_____
_____
_____
_____
_____
_____
_____
_____
_____
_____
_____
_____
_____
_____
_____

Action

_____
_____
_____
_____
_____
_____
_____
_____
_____
_____
_____
_____
_____
_____
_____

Day 22: ATTACHMENTS

We have to be very careful and mindful of who gets attached to us. Make sure that you do not have any leeches that are simply around you for the ride. The definition of a *leech* is "one that preys on another; parasite." There may already be some things you wish to pursue and achieve, but you are being held back. A leech will suck the energy, time, and substance out of your hopes, dreams, and aspirations.

Initially, you may have thought this person had your best interest at heart, but be cautious. There is no need to operate in fear, but it is wise to take inventory of our relationships. We all need mutually beneficial relationships to assist our growth and help us along the way, but there are a few people who only wish to get attached to someone else's dream. Some wish to reap the benefits of a relationship, but they have no desire to contribute to the work. How many times have you had to deal with that one individual who always wants to ride but never wants to contribute any gas money? Continue to be mindful and seek God's wisdom and ask that He surrounds you with people who have your best interest at heart.

THINK IT

Reflection

_____
_____
_____
_____
_____
_____
_____
_____
_____
_____
_____
_____
_____
_____
_____

Action

_____
_____
_____
_____
_____
_____
_____
_____
_____
_____
_____
_____
_____
_____

Day 23: CARRYING THE EXTRA WEIGHT

When do you know to let go? There may be people in your life that always seem to take but never want to give. How long do you hold on to friendships or relationships where you are constantly having to sacrifice your time and energy? That "extra weight" will drain your body and put extra stress on your mind because you do not want to see this person struggle. When do you say, "enough is enough"? You must pay close attention to these types of relationships because people will often take advantage of your willingness to help. At no point in time do you want to be a crutch for someone. It is one thing to genuinely help a friend in their time of need, but it is another thing when that person takes advantage of your kindness.

Any "extra weight" can be a burden and can make it extremely difficult for you to move forward. It is much harder to run a mile while pulling the weight of two, three, or four tires. Extra baggage is easy to get, but it is difficult to lose. Take inventory of your relationships and make sure you are not continuously carrying "extra weight."

THINK IT

Reflection

_____

_____

_____

_____

_____

_____

_____

_____

_____

_____

_____

_____

_____

_____

Action

_____

_____

_____

_____

_____

_____

_____

_____

_____

_____

_____

_____

_____

_____

Day 24: SEASONAL RELATIONSHIPS

Throughout our lives, many people will come and go. At different ages, we experience various tests and go through certain trials that we have absolutely no control over. Oftentimes, this is the time when a particular person walks into our lives. He or she will walk into our lives at the exact time we need someone with their unique qualities. You may think that this relationship will be one that will last forever because the person was there for you in your time of need. Without explanation, this exact person may do or say something that makes absolutely no sense at all. Then, it seems that the relationship is broken, and you are puzzled because the relationship that you thought was meant to last forever is now destroyed. This is defined as a "seasonal relationship."

God has appointed particular people to be a part of your life for only a season, for a particular reason, and no more. You needed them as you changed and grew; therefore, the purpose of that relationship may be to see you through to the next phase of your life. Just as we experience the seasons of fall, winter, spring, and summer, we also experience seasons of growth and change. There is nothing you can do to make some relationships last for this very reason, so thank God for sending them into your life. There will be some lasting relationships as well, but we must recognize and acknowledge that we will experience seasonal relationships. What we must realize is that "we meet certain people on a set date and at a particular time for an appointed reason and season."

Reflection

_____
_____
_____
_____
_____
_____
_____
_____
_____
_____
_____
_____
_____
_____

Action

_____
_____
_____
_____
_____
_____
_____
_____
_____
_____
_____
_____
_____
_____

Day 25: THE SEASON IS CHANGING

Fall is the time of year when our surroundings begin to change. We see lush foliage giving way to brilliant hues. Fall is also the time that the old leaves prepare to be released and make room for new leaves and blooms. It is a time of preparation for what is to come. As fall arrives, the temperature falls, and we are forced to adapt to the environment. We begin to understand the process and necessity of letting go. This is why it is so critical that we do not remain stagnant in our current status. Since the world is constantly changing, we must always remain flexible enough to grow with that change. There are not enormous amounts of guarantees in this world, but each and every year, the seasons must change.

Change is a necessity in life, and if you do not grow during the process, you will get left behind. If the animals are able to recognize that the seasons are changing and that they must migrate to different areas, then we should surely be prepared for the change. Many people have a deep fear of change because of the unknown circumstances that they may have to face. Therefore, I must reiterate that change is crucially important in order to continuously move forward. You would not wear your summer clothes during the freezing temperatures of the winter months because you understand that a change of clothes is necessary. In this same way, we cannot be afraid to alter our lifestyles as we mature with wisdom.

THINK IT

Reflection

_____
_____
_____
_____
_____
_____
_____
_____
_____
_____
_____
_____
_____
_____

Action

_____
_____
_____
_____
_____
_____
_____
_____
_____
_____
_____
_____
_____
_____

Day 26: TIME FOR AN UPGRADE

There comes a time when you become too familiar with your surroundings. The four walls around you seem to be closing in on you, and you need more room to grow. It is time for an upgrade. The words *can't*, *don't*, *won't*, and *impossible* are no longer a part of your life. You do not need anyone to validate your gifts and abilities. When everyone else doubts your dreams, you must remain faithful and committed to excellence.

It does not matter how nice your wardrobe looks if you have not upgraded your mind. You are no longer bound to the mistakes or struggles of previous generations. Success runs through your veins, and it is time for you to reveal the new you. How long will you remain stuck in the past? There is a greater version of you living on the inside of you. You are not who you used to be, and the world needs to see and hear your overcoming story.

THINK IT

Reflection

Action

Day 27: INVEST IN YOURSELF (Part 1)

Real estate, mutual funds, stocks, and bonds are all great assets. However, all these assets go up and down in value over time. Therefore, the best investment that you can make is in the person you see in the mirror because you are your greatest asset. Your mind has the ability to create the largest return on your initial investment — period. The enemy wants to "lower your value" by making you think you are sorry, pitiful, and a mistake. The reason the enemy attacks you is because he wants to bring disunity and confusion into your life and attempt to make you think you have "lost your value."

That's exactly why you need to DIVORCE him immediately. Do not give him authority over your life because he is the father of lies and only desires to kill, steal, and destroy. No matter how bruised, beaten, and abused you may feel, God wants to restore your joy. This type of joy is found in Him and in Him alone. As you begin to further invest in what is already in you, you become one step closer to fulfilling your purpose.

THINK IT

Reflection

_____
_____
_____
_____
_____
_____
_____
_____
_____
_____
_____
_____
_____
_____

Action

_____
_____
_____
_____
_____
_____
_____
_____
_____
_____
_____
_____
_____

Day 28: I'VE FALLEN, AND I MUST GET UP
(Part 1: Where Do I Start?)

What do you do when you continue to make the same mistakes? We all can relate to this topic because every man and woman has some type of weakness. We must first recognize and admit our faults and shortcomings. You cannot overcome what you refuse to identify. We are imperfect human beings, and we are naturally focused on ourselves.

We have to know both our good and bad habits so that we can resist the temptation that consistently challenges us day-to-day. Why? Everybody does not want to see you succeed, so they want to put you in an uncomfortable position to see how you will react to your surroundings. That can be tough when you are in a college or an early workforce environment because you want to enjoy yourself. However, never compromise your morals and values to meet the temporary needs or instant gratifications of another individual or group. At the end of the night, you have to revisit your actions and live with what you see in the mirror. Yes, you have fallen, but you MUST get up. You have been delayed but not denied, bruised but not beaten down, and God wants you to renew your mind, change your mental attitude, take off your old self, and put on a brand new you.

Reflection

_____
_____
_____
_____
_____
_____
_____
_____
_____
_____
_____
_____
_____
_____

Action

_____
_____
_____
_____
_____
_____
_____
_____
_____
_____
_____
_____
_____

Day 29: WHAT IS THE PLAN?

Take five minutes to calculate how much time you spend working for another individual or group. Someone else has already planned your projects at work, your course syllabus, and routine activities at your job. Now take the time to calculate how much time you have spent planning for success over the past one, three, or five months for your next one, three, or five years. Are you planning to succeed?

It's imperative that you invest time in planning for your success. Begin with a brainstorming session in which you write out all of your thoughts, goals, and possibilities in their rawest forms. Do not get caught up in grammar and things makings sense. Instead, think of it as a puzzle that you'll put together later. After your brainstorm is completed take the time to bring clarity to what goes where and the timing of when it needs to happen. Keep this document somewhere easy to access.

When you put your thoughts on paper, you are making a commitment to achieve what you have written. Too many times, we think of great ideas, but they fail to become tangible because we did not properly plan their execution. The car you drive, the outfit you wear, and the TV you watch all began with a plan. If you begin to get discouraged while attempting to achieve this goal, you can always revisit your visual plan. These plans will remind you of your original commitment and keep you motivated as you pursue your dream.

Reflection

_____
_____
_____
_____
_____
_____
_____
_____
_____
_____
_____
_____
_____
_____
_____

Action

_____
_____
_____
_____
_____
_____
_____
_____
_____
_____
_____
_____
_____
_____

Day 30: INVEST IN YOURSELF (Part 2)

Take, at least, ten minutes today to reflect on what you do day-to-day and decide if you are properly investing in your future. Do you spend more time watching TV than you do educating yourself and working toward your own dreams? A lot of the wealthy people that I frequently speak to begin with the end result in mind. It is so easy to speak about what you can't do, frown, and be lazy. However, it takes someone with true character and integrity to steadily get better day after day.

No matter how busy your schedule may be, it is crucial and necessary to spend part of your day alone with the expectation of improving yourself. Why? The world will go on with or without you, and time will not stop for anyone. We often spend 40 percent of our time watching someone else's dream come true (for example: television) and another 40 percent working to make someone else's dream come true (for example: your job). Take action today to invest in yourself, and every day, you should be taking forward steps and getting one step closer to your desired level of achievement. This daily investment can be as simple as reading a book or listening to a podcast to something as complex as seeking a mentor who's achieved the success you see for yourself. Whatever it is, invest in yourself. Your return is guaranteed to be a good one.

THINK IT

Reflection

_____
_____
_____
_____
_____
_____
_____
_____
_____
_____
_____
_____
_____
_____

Action

_____
_____
_____
_____
_____
_____
_____
_____
_____
_____
_____
_____
_____
_____

Day 31: SOMEDAY

When it comes to starting the process of working toward specific goals, how many times have you used the word someday? You may desire to start a business, do some short- or long-term investing, begin exercising, etc., but that word someday is still lingering around and delaying your progress.

Time and time again, you have boldly claimed what you plan on accomplishing. In all honesty, you really meant what you said. However, by attaching that word someday to the end of your statement, you have actually stamped the word delayed on your plans. We often put off the very things that should be top priorities because we get caught up in our busy schedules and daily routines.

Today will be a day of change. Choose one thing that you have been attaching the word someday to in your life. It does not have to be anything major because small or subtle changes can produce major impacts. In one or two sentences, write down what you want to begin to change, but attach the word today to the end of the statement.

Reflection

_____
_____
_____
_____
_____
_____
_____
_____
_____
_____
_____
_____
_____
_____
_____

Action

_____
_____
_____
_____
_____
_____
_____
_____
_____
_____
_____
_____
_____
_____

Day 32: UNDER CONSTRUCTION

On the first day of the month, it is important to begin with the end in mind. When you look at yourself and think about what you are dealing with at this time, it may seem that you have failed. Stress can truly be a burden. For example, school may be getting on your nerves, and the hours at work may not seem to go by fast enough. The statement "the first governs the rest" is a powerful one.

You may have extra stress, such as trouble at school and difficulty at work, because there is one thing in your life that is affecting everything else. One problem can occur at the beginning of your day, and because of it, the rest of your day can be thrown off track. However, your character is not defined by your circumstances and your problem is not bigger than your purpose. You may be waist-deep in a problem, and your range of motion may feel limited, but you must know that there is a way of escape. You need to place a "letter of notice" on top of your current problem and tell the next problem that may come your way that you are "under construction." If a building or website has the label "under construction" on it, people understand why the business is not open. There is a process taking place on the inside that people on the outside looking in may not be able to completely understand.

Change is taking place. Your vision is being stretched, and you are going to a new level in your life. Do not let anyone degrade you with their words due to what they see on the outside because you are "under construction."

Begin with the end in mind and envision yourself going to the next level.

Reflection

_____
_____
_____
_____
_____
_____
_____
_____
_____
_____
_____
_____
_____
_____
_____

Action

_____
_____
_____
_____
_____
_____
_____
_____
_____
_____
_____
_____
_____
_____
_____

Day 33: BROUGHT YOU OUT TO BRING YOU IN

Stop for a moment and think about all the tests, trials, tear-dropping, and traumatizing events that have occurred throughout the course of this year. Only you truly know what you have faced and dealt with so far. Some of us have lost loved ones. Some. Some of us have suffered some form of abuse, and others of us have had to deal with various unexpected events.

Take time to reflect upon what has happened in your life, but do not get stuck in the past. You may have felt abandoned or robbed of life's joy, but God has a light of blessing prepared for the darkness in your life. Although it is dark outside during the night, the darkness is removed with the rising of the sun. We may have to deal with dark and difficult times in our lives, but your current situation is not a permanent place. God brings you out of troublesome situations to bring you closer to his LOVE. When everything else in life has failed to heal your wounds, rely upon God's Word. As he brings you out of your darkness, your character and strength are being increased. There is a divine purpose and plan for what you are going through, and it is not meant to destroy your life.

You are being transformed into a better individual as you come out of your broken place, so trust that your tomorrow will look better than your today.

Reflection

_____

_____

_____

_____

_____

_____

_____

_____

_____

_____

_____

_____

_____

_____

_____

Action

_____

_____

_____

_____

_____

_____

_____

_____

_____

_____

_____

_____

_____

_____

Day 34: LAYING THE FOUNDATION

What are you currently attempting to build? Before a major construction project begins, careful planning must take place, and it is critical that the foundation is laid properly. If there were no blueprints or secured financing, what are the chances of the building being built properly? In the same way, many people are attempting to achieve a successful lifestyle on a weak and insecure foundation. We must invest our time wisely in order to increase the likelihood of making our dreams come true.

Would you want a doctor to perform surgery on you if he or she had not received the proper training? Of course not because the basic foundation of skills has not been acquired. Do not leave achieving your goals solely to chance. Once time has passed, there is truly no going back. You do not want to miss out on great opportunities because of a weak foundation.

Lasting relationships will not endure the test of time if they have solely been built on a physical attraction. Choose today to lay that foundation so that your children's children will also be blessed. The strength of the walls, inner structure, and roofing of a building will not matter if the bottom is weak. Build your career with a solid basis of integrity, wisdom, and a hard work ethic. You may have to destroy some other things first, but it is important to make sure the right foundation is in place.

Reflection

_____
_____
_____
_____
_____
_____
_____
_____
_____
_____
_____
_____
_____
_____

Action

_____
_____
_____
_____
_____
_____
_____
_____
_____
_____
_____
_____
_____

Day 35: SETTING THE STANDARD

A popular saying states, "If you do not stand for something, you will fall for anything." Have you set a standard or level of requirement around certain areas of your life? At some point in time, you may have experienced an awful relationship that left you feeling empty or even unappreciated. Well, you may need or want to call that person and tell them "thank you." That experience simply made you stronger, and now you are even better at recognizing what you do not want in a relationship. Now you are in a position to set the standard, and it is up to you to determine your levels of acceptance. At the same time, because you have set the standard, you have set an example that others must acknowledge and respect. Your friends may not even suggest certain activities for you to participate in because they understand the standards you have in place.

You have one life to live, and you do not have time to lower your standards to fit into the expectations of others. What would the car dealership say if you walked on the lot attempting to purchase a new Mercedes-Benz for $19,000 just because that is the price of a Toyota Camry? In their eyes, that is unacceptable because their standards are in place.

Now it's time to set yours. Raise your standards and do not settle for less.

Reflection

_____
_____
_____
_____
_____
_____
_____
_____
_____
_____
_____
_____
_____
_____

Action

_____
_____
_____
_____
_____
_____
_____
_____
_____
_____
_____
_____
_____
_____
_____

Day 36: THE REAL YOU

What do you think about when you initially meet someone? Did you know that many people form, at least, nine to ten opinions of you in the first seven seconds of your initial conversation? Many of us have acquaintances but lack true friendships because we are afraid of exposing our weaknesses.

Let me tell you that there are hundreds of people we pass by throughout the week who are broken on the inside and seeking authentic relationships. We all have concerns and issues on the inside that we carry around with us every day, and those issues may go unnoticed to a person standing on the outside looking in. Believe it or not, you need a circle of people to get to know the "real you." I may have never laid eyes on you, but I know there is more to you than just a good-looking face and nice clothes.

When you honestly speak from your heart to people, you are releasing an indicator of your inner condition. As a human being, you were not created to be alone, so you need encouraging relationships for support. There are many people who may walk by you and smile while they may be going through the toughest time of their lives. Take notice of how often you walk by a stranger or someone you barely know and halfheartedly ask, "How are you doing?" Also, take notice of how you do not even stick around to hear what they have to say. Be genuine in the words you say and take the time today to let someone know you sincerely care.

Reflection

_____
_____
_____
_____
_____
_____
_____
_____
_____
_____
_____
_____
_____
_____
_____
_____

Action

_____
_____
_____
_____
_____
_____
_____
_____
_____
_____
_____
_____
_____
_____

Day 37: WHAT ARE YOU WILLING TO LIVE WITH?

At times, we ask ourselves, "Why am I still dealing with this situation?" There can be certain people in your life or in a particular situation in your life that continuously linger in your mind, but let me ask you, "What are you willing to live with?"

It is not always the case that we do not know that something or someone is not good for our lives. Oftentimes, we are very aware that we are dealing with an unhealthy situation, yet we do not take the proper action to remove the problem. These stressful areas can be very deceiving. They initially come over to your house to spend some quality time with you. Next, they ask to spend the night, and the next thing you know, they have not left in weeks. Before you know it, they are moving in with no plans of finding a job or contributing to the monthly bills. Gradually, these stressful areas have moved into your life, and because you have become so familiar with their qualities, you decide to just live with them.

It's time to pull out the tape, boxes, and scissors and call the moving company. It is time to clean out some closets and start over. Do not live with the words *broke, misery, stress, depression, lack,* or *jealousy*. You must remove this unwanted waste, so you can make room for what God wants to give you. Think again about what you are willing to live with because, once you let them in, it is ten times harder to get them out.

Reflection

_____
_____
_____
_____
_____
_____
_____
_____
_____
_____
_____
_____
_____
_____

Action

_____
_____
_____
_____
_____
_____
_____
_____
_____
_____
_____
_____
_____
_____
_____

Day 38: WHAT'S YOUR PLATFORM?

I took the time to watch a friend compete in the Miss America Pageant, and something that was very interesting to me was that each contestant had a platform. The various platforms consisted of an issue, program, or personal focus that was meaningful and purpose-driven for each contestant.

While it is great to enjoy life, it is also necessary to focus. What are you dedicated to achieving? What is your personal platform? We are all fascinated with different interests, and in order to take progressive steps, we must make a contribution. Commit your time, energy, and effort to a specific cause that piques your interest and motivates your spirit.

Some of you may think that what you feel passionate about will not make a difference or a significant impact. Our world won't be the same until you take action. You must discover and implement your platform. Future generations are depending on your individual contribution. Do not just stand on the sidelines and watch. Get in the game with a never-quitting attitude. You are here to fulfill a purpose, and you have been designed and equipped for your journey.

Reflection

_____
_____
_____
_____
_____
_____
_____
_____
_____
_____
_____
_____
_____
_____
_____

Action

_____
_____
_____
_____
_____
_____
_____
_____
_____
_____
_____
_____
_____
_____

Day 39: GETTING YOU OFF TRACK

Where has your focus been lately? There are so many distractions that are competing for your attention, especially considering the status of the world today. Family issues, substance abuse, sexual temptations, and financial problems are only a few areas that can cause a lack of focus.

As you pursue career goals and plan for a prosperous future, distractions will obstruct your path. Staying on track was not easy for anyone that came before you, and it definitely will not be easy for you, and it's going to be difficult for those after you. It is your job to keep "driving" toward success, and it is the enemy's job to cause some accidents along your path. He wants you to crash, and he wants your dreams to be completely destroyed with no chances of repair. It all begins by recognizing the enemy's traps, and he only has three tricks that he uses against you: 1) Cravings of the flesh, 2) Lust of the eyes, and 3) Pride (boasting and trying to appear important). If you notice that you are getting slightly off track, make some adjustments. If you have been off track because of a lack of focus, then it is time to revisit your divine game plan.

Reflection

_____

_____

_____

_____

_____

_____

_____

_____

_____

_____

_____

_____

_____

_____

_____

Action

_____

_____

_____

_____

_____

_____

_____

_____

_____

_____

_____

_____

_____

_____

Day 40: ON TRACK

Where do you currently stand with what you set out to accomplish at the beginning of this year? If you have lost some of the initial enthusiasm that you had or have slightly off-course, then it is time to get refreshed. Unfortunately, various obstacles do get in your way, and some troubles make your ride rough, but you must not get off the track. It is time to press forward and drive through. While browsing the internet for information, sometimes the pages do not display properly. However, you do not have to turn the power off on the computer. You just need to refresh the page. In the same way, when life seems to drain you and take your energy, your mind, body, and soul need to be refreshed. Do not allow a few problems in the early part of the year to ruin what God has destined for you in the latter part. Do not get off the track and do not quit on your dream. Grip the steering wheel, roll up your sleeves, and dig deeper. These early trials are only there to prepare you for what is soon to come. If you quit now, you will be abandoning and aborting the process and getting out of position.

Do not let go. Continue to go forward despite what comes against you.

Reflection

Action

Day 41: IT'S ALREADY HERE

What have you been searching for or seeking to find? Oftentimes, when we are looking for answers, we start by looking at external influences, such as family, friends, or co-workers. While it is recommended to seek guidance and be surrounded by wise counsel, you are missing the correct initial step. The initial step is to ask God because, many times, what you are looking for is already in your possession. There are some things inside of you that you have not used, and it is in you comes in the form of untapped gifts. You may not have realized it, but while you were going through those problems and tough situations in your life, wisdom was being sown into your heart.

That problem taught you something, and at the same time, it stretched your capacity. Because of that, you can now face a similar situation with a wiser approach. We must learn to tap into what has been embedded inside of us and draw from it when we are faced with a dilemma. There are certain things that the enemy likes to put in your face, so he can stop you from growing. However, what God has planted cannot be uprooted, so use what you have been given.

With time, you will begin to see your life change for the better.

Reflection

_____
_____
_____
_____
_____
_____
_____
_____
_____
_____
_____
_____
_____
_____

Action

_____
_____
_____
_____
_____
_____
_____
_____
_____
_____
_____
_____
_____
_____

Day 42: TAKE YOUR CONTROL BACK

Regardless of the city and state in which you currently reside, great opportunities are present. The question is: Are you prepared and in a position to take advantage of those opportunities?

What good is it to go through the steps of finding and purchasing your desired vehicle, if you are just going to hand over the keys to someone else so they can do the driving? He or she is in the driver's seat while you are seating in the passenger's seat. Whether it is your car or not, that person controls where you are going. Is someone else in the driver's seat of your life?

We live in an ever-changing environment; therefore, we must be in control of our lives in order to take full advantage of all the opportunities that come our way. If things seem out of order, take your control back. Do not passively go through life waiting for someone else to give you a handout. Rather than standing on the sidelines and watching the game, go make it happen. What are the chances of making it happen if you are afraid to get in the game? Each day provides a new opportunity to write a new and greater chapter in your life. Without control, your risk increases, and you leave your future to chance.

No one can beat you at being you.

Reflection

_____
_____
_____
_____
_____
_____
_____
_____
_____
_____
_____
_____
_____
_____

Action

_____
_____
_____
_____
_____
_____
_____
_____
_____
_____
_____
_____
_____
_____

Day 43: NEGATIVITY IS CONTAGIOUS

There is a reason that negativity is published and broadcasted more quickly than any positive news. Simply put, negativity is contagious, and a lot of people are drawn to negative information. For some, it is entertaining to hear that someone has made a mistake in life and failed to live up to their expectations. Bad news is good news for those who desire to see you fail. It may be detrimental to you, but it is entertaining to others.

Have you ever noticed how gossip about good things moves at a snail's pace, but gossip about negative information spreads like wildfire? Do you always have control over what people think or say about you? You certainly do not. At the same time, we must realize that, in order to continue to progressively move forward, we must move away from negative people and situations. It is not always easy to tell who is on your side and who is not. Be mindful of who is talking in your ear because you do not want negative information to go into your mind. Eventually, it will begin to leak out of your mouth. You do not have to conform to the people who are creating a negative environment. You can break the mold and set the example. Too many people are afraid to speak up and not be like everyone else because of what others might think. Put yourself in the position of the person that is being spoken about negatively and do your best to shed some light on his or her dark situation.

Reflection

_____
_____
_____
_____
_____
_____
_____
_____
_____
_____
_____
_____
_____
_____
_____

Action

_____
_____
_____
_____
_____
_____
_____
_____
_____
_____
_____
_____
_____
_____
_____
_____

Day 44: WHY ARE YOU CALLING ME OUT?

How awkward does it make you feel when someone calls you out? When you least expect it, someone puts you on the spot, and you find yourself in an unexpected position. Today, you are being called out. You are being called out because it's time to push yourself beyond your normal boundaries.

We are living in a time when it's no longer acceptable to casually and passively live life as if it's business as usual. Pay attention to what is going on in the news and around the world, and you will see that the world needs your strengths and abilities. Do not sit on your gifts. Long life is not always guaranteed, no matter how healthy or young you may feel.

I'm calling you out and challenging you to take a more active role. It may initially feel uncomfortable, but being out of your comfort zone pushes you and stretches your possibilities.

Decide today that you are not going to just sit on the sideline.

Reflection

_____
_____
_____
_____
_____
_____
_____
_____
_____
_____
_____
_____
_____

Action

_____
_____
_____
_____
_____
_____
_____
_____
_____
_____
_____
_____
_____

Day 45: I'VE FALLEN AND I MUST GET UP (Part 2)

How do you get up from your fallen position? How do you get up off the floor and get back on the right path? Well, I honestly believe that a big reason we are in our current positions is because we are fighting an internal battle. Again, we cannot overcome what we dodo not identify, so let's look further. Our hearts, minds, and souls are being tugged in many different directions as we seek to please ourselves and fulfill the expectations of others. When you have fallen, you must move in only one direction, and that is forward. If you dwell on your mistakes and magnify the problem, rather than focus on the solution, the results will be disappointing.

Understand that, no matter what you are currently facing, YOU ARE NOT ALONE! Many people have lived and overcome what you are currently dealing with. You must draw strength from their victories. I must reiterate that you are not alone. Do not let the devil make you feel isolated and alone because you will be fighting a losing battle. He wants to push you into a dark corner, make you feel as if you've lost your value, degrade you, and expose your faults. Well, show me one man or woman who is perfect. You fail when you quit; however, you are not a quitter. Every great person has achieved phenomenal success after initially losing a few battles. So even though you may have lost a few battles, there is more to your story.

Reflection

Action

Day 46: GET BACK IN THE GAME...AND GROW UP

Whenever you return to a place that you have not been in a while, things may seem a bit out of order. Sometimes it may be difficult to get back into the groove of things. You attempt to recall how things were before, but it is somewhat difficult. If you feel a bit uncomfortable, that is good. You should feel out of place. You have grown up and matured beyond many childish activities.

One way that we often hinder ourselves from moving forward is by returning to a "familiar place." We fail to get better because we are too comfortable doing the same old routine. As you learn from past experiences and others' mistakes, you should be improving your character. Do not get me wrong. You should definitely enjoy whatever age you are now. However, if you are continuously repeating activities that previously put you in an awkward position or got you into trouble, it is time to grow up. Learn from your mistakes and be an example for others.

BE IT

Reflection

_____
_____
_____
_____
_____
_____
_____
_____
_____
_____
_____
_____
_____
_____
_____

Action

_____
_____
_____
_____
_____
_____
_____
_____
_____
_____
_____
_____
_____
_____

Day 47: ARE YOU LISTENING?

How many times have you told someone, "You are hearing me, but are you listening?" There is a key difference between the two because listening requires an attentive ear, along with some comprehension. You can "hear" what someone is saying, then walk away without comprehending one word of what they have just said. However, the art of listening requires more effort from your ears and less effort from your mouth. You are, indeed, a uniquely created individual, but you have two ears and one mouth for a reason because you should strive to listen twice as much as you speak.

Build meaningful relationships by attentively listening to the needs and concerns of others. Sometimes, you get so caught up in talking and trying to get your point across that others barely hear or comprehend what you are saying, and they t are just waiting for you to quit talking, so they can say what is on their minds. This creates an unhealthy conversation, and in the end, nothing is settled.

Many of us love to talk, but we are poor listeners. Do not just hear what God has to say about your life and walk away unchanged. Listen to the wisdom that He will place in your heart, and He will guide your path, regardless of the uncertainty of the situation.

Reflection

_____
_____
_____
_____
_____
_____
_____
_____
_____
_____
_____
_____
_____
_____
_____

Action

_____
_____
_____
_____
_____
_____
_____
_____
_____
_____
_____
_____
_____
_____
_____
_____

Day 48: INCREASING FAITH

What is your current faith level? Oftentimes, we deal with the obstacles and problems we face by worrying about and overanalyzing them. While all of us must deal with different situations at different times in our lives, we still have to operate with faith. When you go to crank up your car, you already have enough faith that it is going to start without even thinking twice about it. Sometimes, we put more faith in money, family, friends, and our jobs than we put in God. How can you trust that your car will crank up every morning but not have faith that God can calm the storms you are battling within your life each and every day?

By increasing our levels of faith, we can amazingly reduce the levels of stress, headaches, and worry in our lives. We often operate backward because we will first look at how big our problem is and then look for an answer that is big enough to solve it. Switch that around today by trusting God first because He has been handling problems like yours for many years now, and He has a flawless track record.

Reflection

_____
_____
_____
_____
_____
_____
_____
_____
_____
_____
_____
_____
_____
_____
_____

Action

_____
_____
_____
_____
_____
_____
_____
_____
_____
_____
_____
_____
_____
_____
_____
_____

Day 49: BE MINDFUL

Be very mindful of who you take advice from when you are in a desperate situation. It is important to remember this because you are in a vulnerable position, and everyone you speak to does not want you to recover from your current position. It is extremely difficult for someone to teach you something if they have not experienced it themselves. Just be mindful of people who talk too much and try to tell you how you should live your life. Before you take your problems to your closest friend or family member, ask God.

Wise counsel and sound advice can be very helpful when you are seeking clarity. This is why it is important to evaluate the values of the people who are closest to you. If you are permitting them to offer you guidance, then you want to make sure they are pointing you in the right direction. You do not have to accept the advice of everyone, nor do you have to live based on their opinions. There is a great benefit to having the right people in the right positions in your life. Take inventory of who is around you, and do not be afraid to make tough decisions. What you do today will largely impact the way you live tomorrow.

Reflection

Action

Day 50: CAN I HAVE YOUR ATTENTION PLEASE?

What gets your attention? What is it that makes you turn your head and look twice or that one thing that so often stays on your mind? I'm sure there are a number of answers. However, what we need to begin analyzing is whether or not those things should be receiving our attention.

No matter who or where you are, we all make individual decisions, whether it is right or wrong. No one always makes the right decisions, but we all must learn to educate ourselves on why we made those bad judgments. We learn some of the best lessons of our lives from the mistakes we make. Do not let anyone tell you that you should be afraid to make a mistake. What we must learn to do is focus our attention on ideas and circumstances that add to and multiply our lives, not subtract and divide. I've never met a millionaire who got there by sitting on the couch and watching TV for four to six hours a day, so be mindful of what you allow to "get your attention."

Reflection

Action

Day 51: CAN YOU STAND THE RAIN?

People have different feelings about how the rain affects their day. Some dread the fact that they have to get wet, while some relax because the rain creates a calming effect, and many will be upset because it slows down their day. Just in case you have ever had these thoughts, let's look at it from a different perspective.

Oftentimes, we go through dry spells in our lives where things just do not go our way. You feel separated from those closest to you, and you feel drained because your hard work is not paying off. Finally, here comes the rain. Whether you knew it or not during your dry spell, you were just sowing seeds and getting the ground ready for your blessing.

A farmer must first prepare the ground and plant seeds before he sees a harvest. While all this is happening, the rain is being formed in the clouds. Just when you feel you cannot take it anymore and you are thirsty for a breakthrough, the rain pours and waters all the seeds that you have planted. The rain nourishes and replenishes every seed that you thought was going to waste, so, s the next time you look up in the sky and see those dark clouds, GET READY! You are growing closer to your breakthrough, and God is preparing you for the right time so that he can pour out his blessings on your life.

Reflection

Action

Day 52: HAVE YOU EVER BEEN SET UP?

Has anyone ever put you in an awkward position in his or her attempts to make you look bad? Do others hate on you because you got it going on? Well, I'm going to let you know that you should be thanking those people for all the pain they tried to cause in your life. Why? Because no matter what they tried to do to you, God had your back. They lied on you, tried to drag your name through the mud, and almost caused you to quit, but it didn't work. You were delayed but not denied, and you lived to fight another day. They didn't even know it, but they were SETTING YOU UP to strengthen your character. A setup is only a setback if you allow it to defeat you. You can also turn that setback into a stepping stone as you advance to a new level. Do not allow what you are going through to set you back.

Pain is a great indicator that you are getting closer to your breakthrough. Most people would have quit if they went through half of what you have been through during your lifetime. Use your survivor story to help someone else get through their hard times because that is what it is all about. So use those setups as motivation and as sources of empowerment as you strengthen the quality of your character.

Reflection

_____
_____
_____
_____
_____
_____
_____
_____
_____
_____
_____
_____
_____
_____

Action

_____
_____
_____
_____
_____
_____
_____
_____
_____
_____
_____
_____
_____
_____

Day 53: GLANCE BACK

It's a good feeling when you sit down with some of your friends and reminisce about past times. During the conversation, you may discuss some good things, some bad, and a few things in the middle that you would prefer to forget. If you looked back over a relationship that has survived the test of time, you will find more than just a few memories.

Take a look at where you are right now. Do you feel that you have accomplished what you planned to do a few months or years ago? Well, just in case you have not, you have to look at the other side of the coin. You may have faced some true hardships in your life, but the truth is you lived to tell your story. The next time there is a mountain in your way that seems too big to overcome, glance back. Do not look back because then you would be focusing on your past. However, if you glance back, you will see some victories. Some situations in your past were too big for you, so God stepped in to release the weight. Glance back and look at all the things you have overcome and use that fuel to motivate you to face your next battle. Draw strength from your past accomplishments and move forward with courage.

Reflection

_____
_____
_____
_____
_____
_____
_____
_____
_____
_____
_____
_____
_____
_____
_____

Action

_____
_____
_____
_____
_____
_____
_____
_____
_____
_____
_____
_____
_____
_____
_____

Day 54: WHY WORRY?

Fear is the root of all worry; however, fear and faith cannot intermingle or live in the same house because they do not get along. When it comes to fear, you have two options: 1) fight or 2) flee. You may have lost some battles throughout your life, but since you survived to read this message, it tells me you are a fighter.

As soon as you start panicking because you think time is up, God releases your blessing right on time because it's according to HIS TIMING. God can and will set you up for your blessing. Unfortunately, some people do not want to see you succeed, and everyone around you is not on your side. It's sad, but some people see more in you than you see in yourself. Stop looking around because the WEALTH is already inside you. The enemy wants you to worry because he wants to cause chaos, disorder, and confusion in your life. Again, fear produces worry, and fear and faith cannot coexist peacefully. Choose today to have faith, despite the fear.

Reflection

_____
_____
_____
_____
_____
_____
_____
_____
_____
_____
_____
_____
_____
_____
_____

Action

_____
_____
_____
_____
_____
_____
_____
_____
_____
_____
_____
_____
_____
_____

Day 55: ARE YOU EQUIPPED WITH ENOUGH?

Do you have what it takes to achieve great success? Do you have the ambition, self-confidence, and work ethic to create a prosperous future? Only you hold the answers. If you do not initially have enough confidence in yourself, why should anyone else place confidence in your abilities?

Many of us have allowed the mistakes of our past to limit our potential while holding us hostage. We cannot allow previous decisions to dictate our future. Many people have already lost half the battle before they even take a step onto the battlefield. Every day, we face battles that have the intent of destroying great opportunities for success. That is why you must have relentless faith and recognize that no problem is bigger than God. You are not maximizing your gifts by attempting to walk in the shoes of another individual. No one can beat you at being you, and we do not need you to be a cheap counterfeit of anyone else. Even if it has not yet been discovered, you must be fully confident that you are already equipped with what you need to fulfill your purpose. There is a wealth of abundance inside of you, and only you can unlock the treasure chest of overflowing favor.

BE IT

Reflection

Action

Day 56: LET IT GO

How do you deal with your built-up emotions throughout the day? After having a tough day, how do you release your anger, frustration, or disappointments? We all need some way to vent in order to release our various inner thoughts. The problem for many of us is that we have these feelings, but we are not sure how to express them properly. Men and women vent their feelings in different ways, but regardless of how we vent our feelings, it is crucially important to do so. That way, you can move on with your day. Sporting activities, reading, speaking to a true friend, or journaling are just a few of the ways to release your feelings.

When you always hold everything in, you are only sweeping your trash under the carpet. The problem is, from an outside perspective, the floor may appear to be clean, but there is built-up trash underneath the rug. Eventually what you have built up over time will reveal itself in the same way that, one day, someone is going to look under that rug and see how much trash has been collected. It's up to you to find the best way for you to vent. Regardless of how it's done, make sure it happens today.

Reflection

_____
_____
_____
_____
_____
_____
_____
_____
_____
_____
_____
_____
_____
_____

Action

_____
_____
_____
_____
_____
_____
_____
_____
_____
_____
_____
_____
_____
_____

Day 57: IS IT MONDAY AGAIN?

Why do some people dread Monday mornings so much? It's actually an extremely vital part of the week because the first governs the rest. Your attitude, thoughts, and behaviors set the atmosphere for the rest of the week. When you open your eyes, the first words that come out of your mouth should be words of encouragement. You woke up to see another day and a lot of people cannot say the same.

Some of you may believe you have nothing to be happy about, but you actually do. There's a key difference between happiness and joy. Your happiness is based on your external circumstances, which you may have no control over. However, your joy is internal. This internal joy is something that the world cannot take away. You should have inner joy, no matter what the world is doing. We must learn to be at peace with ourselves and have the self-confidence to know that we are more than conquerors. Remember that what you do on Monday sets the tone for the rest of your week.

Reflection

_____

_____

_____

_____

_____

_____

_____

_____

_____

_____

_____

_____

_____

_____

Action

_____

_____

_____

_____

_____

_____

_____

_____

_____

_____

_____

_____

_____

_____

Day 58: THE CLOCK IS TICKING

How many times have you found yourself continuously checking the clock in class or at work? There are many other things you would prefer to be doing, and you are just waiting for it all to end. Well, while you are watching the clock, time is not watching you. Whether you maximize your time or lay around on the couch watching television, time will pass.

You do not have time to watch the clock. Find a way to make the best out of the situation. No one does what he or she wants to do 100 percent of the time. Even the most famous faces you admire often have to deal with circumstances that are not so interesting. However, it is a part of life, and we must learn to not focus on situations that are out of our control.

You can buy and sell a lot of items in this world, but one thing that you cannot buy back is time. Yesterday is already gone, and the choices you make today determine how you will live tomorrow. Stop continuously glancing at the clock, it's still ticking. Remember to stay focused, work smart, and make the best out of the situation.

Reflection

Action

Day 59: DON'T LOOK DOWN, LOOK UP

One of the first signs of sadness, depression, or disappointment is a head hanging low. When we face some of life's greatest struggles, we automatically begin to drop our heads and look down. However, it is time for a change because we have been looking in the wrong direction. Your help in your time of need comes from above.

The result you received may have been an unexpected outcome, but you can recover. When you begin to look up, you are reminding yourself that you are capable of a turnaround. Take a moment to analyze your current condition so that you can learn from the experience, but do not dwell on an uncontrollable outcome. Too many people hinder themselves from a quicker recovery because their minds will not allow them to move past what has already occurred. If you feel you have hit rock bottom, you are already in a position to look up. Great opportunities are awaiting your progressive steps, so you do not have time to constantly feel defeated. Choose to not look back or down because it is time to look up and move forward.

Reflection

_____
_____
_____
_____
_____
_____
_____
_____
_____
_____
_____
_____
_____
_____

Action

_____
_____
_____
_____
_____
_____
_____
_____
_____
_____
_____
_____
_____
_____
_____

Day 60: ACCEPTING YOUR CALLING

At this point in your life, where do you feel you ought to be? Are you behind, on time, or already working ahead of schedule? Think about where you are as you are reading this message and examine your daily lifestyle. Realize your calling can come at any moment and at any point in time. You may realize your calling before you finish reading this message. It truly does not matter whether you are sitting, standing, crying, or joyful. You can be in your car, at work, or in class. At the same time, you can attempt to run from what you know you are supposed to be doing, but in doing so, you are only delaying your prosperity. The longer you wait, the longer you delay your blessing, which results in missed opportunities.

In the back of your mind, you may already know your purpose, but you may not feel you are ready. Timing is very critical, but if you know that your season is now and you are still procrastinating, you are falling behind. Be thankful for your gift. I once heard one of my favorite speakers say, "Do not complain or waste time because someone else could take the hand you have been dealt and win with it."

Reflection

_____
_____
_____
_____
_____
_____
_____
_____
_____
_____
_____
_____
_____
_____

Action

_____
_____
_____
_____
_____
_____
_____
_____
_____
_____
_____
_____
_____
_____

LIVE IT

Day 61: UNDERSTAND YOUR POSITION

In a multimillion-dollar corporation, many workers work throughout the day. Within the makeup of the organization, there may be regular associates, managers, HR personnel, and presidents. While all these positions help the daily operations of the company, there is only one CEO. With the CEO position comes authority, leadership, and true responsibility. So where do you fit into this picture?

Regardless of your situation, you must understand your position. God created you to be the head and not the tail, above and not beneath, and He has given you dominion over your circumstances. While the enemy wants to keep you down by keeping you bound to a discouraging situation, you have to let him know your position. All of you have kingship and royalty running through your veins because you come from an Almighty Creator. The circumstance you are facing is only temporary, and within that storm is a strengthening tool that is going to be used to build your character to take on further responsibility. No longer do you have to accept discouraging words from negative people. Your future is waiting on the decisions that you make today.

Reflection

_____

_____

_____

_____

_____

_____

_____

_____

_____

_____

_____

_____

_____

_____

Action

_____

_____

_____

_____

_____

_____

_____

_____

_____

_____

_____

_____

_____

_____

Day 62: THIS TIME NEXT YEAR

W hat is going to be happening at this very same hour and day next year? Have you thought about what you desire to have accomplished by that time? You may be going through tough circumstances, so you may be hoping that they will just go away. They are consuming your time and energy, and you may not know how much more of it you can take.

You can turn your situation around through faith, perseverance, and an unwilling-to-quit attitude. Believe that, at this same time next year, you are going to be in a better position. Believe that, at this very same date next year, everyone around you will be able to notice that a change has occurred in your life.

Oftentimes, we do not get our preferred outcome because we have failed to claim our success in advance. The words that you are speaking about your current situation have more power than you may think. Do not just take my word for it. Try it yourself. You have absolutely nothing to lose, but you have unlimited opportunities to gain. Write down where you desire to be at this same time next year and work at it on a daily basis. This time next year, you can look back at what you wrote down and determine your progress.

Reflection

_____
_____
_____
_____
_____
_____
_____
_____
_____
_____
_____
_____
_____
_____
_____

Action

_____
_____
_____
_____
_____
_____
_____
_____
_____
_____
_____
_____
_____
_____
_____

Day 63: WHO GETS THE CREDIT?

What if you originated a new idea or made a significant impact to a school or work project but someone else got the credit? Some of you have been in this position. How many times have you willingly helped out a friend or family member, but in the end, they were ungrateful? It's not that you were expecting anything big in return, but you would have liked to have, at least, received a "thank you." Is it that difficult for them to show some type of sign that they appreciated the fact that you took time out of your busy schedule to assist them in their time of need?

We do not always give credit where credit is due. A lot of times, when we are in a bad predicament, we will go to our friends, family members, teachers, or counselors before we take our problems to God. Have we forgotten that time and time again, God has met our deepest needs, even when we did not originally recognize his mercy and grace that works in our lives? We tried everything else, and when everything seemed to be failing, we, all of a sudden, received an answer and made it out of harm's way. It was not a coincidence. Unlike us human beings, God does not want our credit to boost His ego or sense of accomplishment. He desires to fill our hearts with His unfailing Word. Of course, we are all imperfect and fall short sometimes, but let's give credit where credit is due. Your plans will prosper, and your vision will be fulfilled only if you are willing to receive His love.

Reflection

_____
_____
_____
_____
_____
_____
_____
_____
_____
_____
_____
_____
_____
_____

Action

_____
_____
_____
_____
_____
_____
_____
_____
_____
_____
_____
_____
_____
_____

Day 64: EXCUSES

There are many people in this world who are filled with extraordinary talents and natural gifts. However, many of these same individuals have not reached their potential because of various excuses. Every time you use excuses, you are using your words as a scapegoat to get yourself out of taking action. Millions of people have walked the Earth and had brilliant ideas and inventions, but they never became tangible products because the excuses they used delayed the process.

Do not let your youthful days pass you by without taking the time to use your untapped gifts. As you get older, you will find yourself in a better position physically, spiritually, and financially because you did not use an abundance of excuses. If there has been something that you have desired to do for quite some time, take the time to plan, strategize, and act on the idea.

Reflection

_____

_____

_____

_____

_____

_____

_____

_____

_____

_____

_____

_____

_____

_____

Action

_____

_____

_____

_____

_____

_____

_____

_____

_____

_____

_____

_____

_____

Day 65: AN AUTHENTIC REALIZATION

When I was growing up, I was a true basketball fan. My friends and I used to buy our favorite players' jerseys, and we would brag and boast about who had purchased the best players' jerseys. After going back and forth for months and months, we finally got the truth. One of my closest friends came to school with an authentic NBA player's jersey, just like they wear in the league, which was clearly special compared to our regular cotton jerseys. From that day forward, we could recognize the real from the fake.

Too many people are walking around bragging and boasting about who they are and what they can do. You have to be true to yourself and realize that the last thing the world needs is another pretender. The longer you put on an act for the crowd, the longer you will continue to hurt on the inside. The world needs to see the real you, and if your friends cannot accept who you really are, then it is time to find some new friends. Do not attempt to cover up your pain because you will only prolong the healing process that you truly need. Release your emotions. Pray about it. Cry a little if you need to. Laugh a lot if you must, but do not continue to pretend to be something you are not.

Have an authentic talk with God and know that He desires the very best for your life.

Reflection

Action

Day 66: AMMUNITION

What if you kept a record of all the words you used throughout the day? What if you handed that record to a total stranger? What would they think about you after reading those words?

Day after day, you subconsciously speak words out of your mouth that make much more of an impact than you think. Your words stem from your thoughts, which originate in your heart. The enemy listens to your words and uses them to slip deceiving thoughts into your mind when you least expect it. All you're doing is giving him ammunition to use against you.

While growing up, you may have heard your parents use phrases that you eventually adopted. They spoke negative results over their situations before they even knew what they were about to face. From having enough resources to pay bills to discouragement before trying something new, even to the extent of just writing something off as "this is just the way things are", their battles were already lost in their thinking process. This explains why we often need to unlearn some of the ways that we have been taught. It takes the same amount of energy to speak positively as it does to speak negatively, so be mindful of the ammunition you are giving the enemy.

Words are too powerful to be used lightly, so do your best to guard your mouth. Many times, we say more by saying less.

LIVE IT

Reflection

_____
_____
_____
_____
_____
_____
_____
_____
_____
_____
_____
_____
_____
_____
_____

Action

_____
_____
_____
_____
_____
_____
_____
_____
_____
_____
_____
_____
_____
_____
_____

Day 67: UNTAPPED OPPORTUNITIES

There are many things that the naked eye is not able to see. Some opportunities can only be found by using your mind, and that allows you to see opportunities that others fail to discover. There are defining moments in our lives that allow us to see Jesus as He is (He reveals himself),. Whether through meeting someone admirable or participating in something you've only dreamed of, you never forget that time. When He truly reveals himself, you cannot deny Him or go back to how you were before.

Along with seeing opportunities in your mind, great things are also recognized by listening to your heart. In your heart lies PASSION, which is built around our natural, God-given talents and abilities. That is why I know when you tap into your gifts and that passion is there, at some point, you will discover your purpose. You cannot look at what others have been able to accomplish and desire what they have acquired. Once you discover your purpose, you will be so busy fulfilling it that you will not have time to desire what someone else possesses. Whether you have a relationship with God or not, in your moments of hardship, ask Him to reveal Himself and pray that He will not leave any gifts undiscovered or unfulfilled. Don't be surprised at what comes up, God certainly isn't. Remain open to what's possible.

Reflection

Action

Day 68: WHAT ARE YOU WAITING FOR?

Something has been on your mind, and it's been tugging at your heart. It has been calling for your attention, but you have been letting the predator called "procrastination" eat away at your time. Hour after hour and day after day, you spend too much time consumed with what others expect you to do.

If your days are similar to a hamster running on a wheel, circle after circle but no progression, then it's time for a wake-up call. The next time your alarm clock goes off, it is not only reminding you that it's time to wake up. It's, also, letting you know that it's time to stop sleeping on your passion. You have prolonged walking toward your goals long enough, and the last thing you want to do is miss your season to use your gifts.

Every time you hear any type of alarm or loud ring going off, it should remind you of your wake-up call. Not only are you delaying your dreams, but you are also cheating others. No one is the best at everything, so it is important that we use our talents to be a blessing to others. You may have thought your abilities were only about you, but your purpose is a lot bigger than you could ever imagine. Do not lose out on this divine opportunity to create a masterpiece for success.

Reflection

_____

_____

_____

_____

_____

_____

_____

_____

_____

_____

_____

_____

_____

_____

_____

_____

Action

_____

_____

_____

_____

_____

_____

_____

_____

_____

_____

_____

_____

_____

_____

_____

_____

_____

Day 69: WHO'S THE GREATEST?

Who are you preparing yourself to be over the next five, ten, or twenty years? A path must be chosen, so where do you see yourself ending up? Some of the most memorable leaders of our time claimed their greatness long before it came to pass. If you do not have complete confidence in your dreams, why should anyone take the time to invest in your future?

Unfortunately, other people often see more in you than you see in yourself. That could be a problem if you allow them to destroy your dreams, but it can also propel you to significant heights of accomplishment if you channel their words in the right direction. Speak about your dreams with boldness and authority so that your passion transfers to the hearts of others.

So who's the greatest? In your chosen field or profession, there is a window of opportunity that can enable you to truly make a remarkable impact. Your words should be full of life, even if the pressures of disappointment attempt to creep in your back door. The greatest fighters are found when they are faced with life's greatest obstacles. Dreams are birthed and destroyed right on the battlefield of your mind, so release those deceiving thoughts today.

Again, who's the greatest? You can be.

Reflection

_____
_____
_____
_____
_____
_____
_____
_____
_____
_____
_____
_____
_____
_____

Action

_____
_____
_____
_____
_____
_____
_____
_____
_____
_____
_____
_____
_____
_____

Day 70: WHEN YOU THINK NO ONE IS LOOKING

We are constantly under the watchful eyes of others. Our good actions, mistakes and everyday living are all on public display and under the scrutiny of those we interact with on a daily basis. However, no matter what they think or say about you, it is up to you to remain truthful to yourself.

I heard one of my favorite actors say, "It doesn't matter what they are calling you, what truly matters is what you answer to." Believe it or not, regardless of your status, occupation, or level of education, you are always being watched. We often think that we are getting away with certain activities because they are not initially exposed. None of us are exempt from sins or temptations, so we must pray for wise discernment with our decision making. No human being has the authority to judge your actions or condemn you. If someone is constantly reminding you of your faults, then it is time to reevaluate that relationship.

Today, as you look in the mirror, do a self-evaluation, and make a decision that, with God's help, you are going to make better decisions. Set the example for your friends, family, co-workers, and classmates. Since they have their eyes on you anyway, leave a lasting impression in their minds.

Successful living is contagious.

LIVE IT

Reflection

Action

Day 71: GETTING TOO COMFORTABLE

In your home, you may have a place like a couch or bed that is extremely comfortable. Once you are in this place of comfort, it relaxes you, and for long periods of time, you have no desire to move. Because you are so accustomed to how it feels, it would be extremely difficult to replace this comfortable setting.

Many of us have become so familiar with our daily routines, settings, and ways of life that change seems too risky. If we lived in perfectly comfortable environments, there would be no motivation or drive toward advancement. Make sure you have not become so accustomed to your current surroundings that you are now stagnant. In order to be successful in your selected area of interest or profession, it is critical that you stay up-to-date with your environment. Comfort births complacency and becoming complacent deprives you of the fulfillment that comes from winning daily battles and striving for your long-term goals. Analyze your current status and take a deeper look at any areas of familiarity or complacency in your life.

Do not allow your comfort to suffocate your drive and ambition. While being uncomfortable is often unsettling, it is necessary to experience true change in your life.

Reflection

_____

_____

_____

_____

_____

_____

_____

_____

_____

_____

_____

_____

_____

Action

_____

_____

_____

_____

_____

_____

_____

_____

_____

_____

_____

_____

_____

_____

Day 72: DON'T PUT WORDS IN MY MOUTH

How many times have you been in a situation where someone felt that they had to speak for you, or they decided to tell you what they thought you should say? Did you speak up for yourself, or did you allow their words to speak for you?

Regardless of someone else's position, occupation, income, or education, you are not inferior. Some people will say certain things to you to see how far you will allow them to go. God has already equipped you with the tools he deemed necessary for you to have, and unless he has given you an interpreter, you need to speak up for yourself. No one can go into your mind, pull out your each and every thought, and speak on your behalf. When you are too passive, it is often interpreted as being weak. Some of us need to stop allowing other people to tell us what we should and should not say and speak with a little more boldness. It is not so much what we say but how we are saying it. Speaking with confidence lets the other person know that you mean what you say and you are not to be taken lightly. Do not allow someone else's words to push your thoughts around. Your voice matters. Be authentic and stand in truth.

Reflection

_____
_____
_____
_____
_____
_____
_____
_____
_____
_____
_____
_____
_____
_____

Action

_____
_____
_____
_____
_____
_____
_____
_____
_____
_____
_____
_____
_____
_____

Day 73: WHERE IS YOUR ANCHOR?

Do you have one thing in your life that keeps you anchored? The taller the tree grows, the deeper the roots must also grow in order for the tree to be firmly planted in the ground. If the tree had short roots, it could easily be uprooted by the slightest wind or the smallest storm.

So, again, how deep are your roots? Does a certain obstacle or the mere sign of a particular problem cause you to be shaken or turned upside down? You may look at the struggles in your life as simply hard times that are merely circumstances you must face. However, our true struggles are really great indicators of the calling and purpose for our lives. The greater your storm, the greater your destiny. You must begin to look at your struggles as an opportunity for character development. As you grow older, your character should also mature because you are no longer thinking as a child. Problems that used to disturb you will now look smaller because your mind has been strengthened. Analyze where your anchor is currently placed and make sure you are rooted in a strong foundation.

LIVE IT

Reflection

_____
_____
_____
_____
_____
_____
_____
_____
_____
_____
_____
_____
_____
_____
_____

Action

_____
_____
_____
_____
_____
_____
_____
_____
_____
_____
_____
_____
_____
_____

Day 74: JUST A LITTLE FURTHER

How close are you to achieving your victory? The battle you are currently facing has stood strong in your path, but you have persevered through to the end. In many cases, right when you feel like giving up, you will find yourself in a critical position where you need to push a little harder. Right when your situation seems unconquerable and impossible to defeat, take one more step forward. So many people give up right before they receive the greatest breakthrough of their lives. You go through so many tests throughout life, and it is your responsibility to not settle for the C-grade and not stop until you receive the A-grade.

On your journey toward success, it may seem that the final victory has evaded you. However, when faced with opposition, the AVERAGE will quit, the GOOD will occasionally win, but the GREAT will knock down the doors of defeat. and make a way for others to follow. There is a great champion living inside your soul. If you quit now, you may miss out on one of the greatest opportunities to make a true impact. So push a little harder for a little longer, and you will receive the benefits of your persevering passion toward success.

Reflection

_____
_____
_____
_____
_____
_____
_____
_____
_____
_____
_____
_____
_____
_____
_____

Action

_____
_____
_____
_____
_____
_____
_____
_____
_____
_____
_____
_____
_____
_____
_____
_____

Day 75: I'M TIRED

Our version of the word tired is very different from what previous generations have called it. The word tired comes out of our mouths automatically when we are not feeling 100 percent. Sometimes, I wonder if we even have a right to use that word. We take a few classes and work a few hours a day, and we feel tired. Do not get me wrong because I know many of us have serious responsibilities. However, oftentimes, there are a select few that complain if they face the slightest obstacle.

Previous generations have worked hard to pave a way so that you and I would have a better chance of achieving success. Do not take their hard work for granted. Sometimes, we need to be reminded of what other people went through for us so that we will be more appreciative of their sacrifices. Stop using words just because you need something to say and be more cautious of the words that come out of your mouth. When you think you feel tired, remind yourself of what someone did for you, and push a little harder.

Reflection

_____
_____
_____
_____
_____
_____
_____
_____
_____
_____
_____
_____
_____
_____

Action

_____
_____
_____
_____
_____
_____
_____
_____
_____
_____
_____
_____
_____
_____

Day 76: FACING OPPOSITION

What do you do when the obstacle you are facing seems impossible to overcome? It seems that you have tried everything, but nothing appears to be working. You may feel as if you are out of options, and you are not sure whether you should look to the right or left. Well, your answer is only a prayer away.

No matter how bad the situation may seem, Keep Fighting. The keyword in the previous statement is *seem*. Your situation may *seem* to be great, but one of the keys to experiencing change is to shift your focus. There is a fighter deep down inside of you that can only be released through FAITH. Stop magnifying your problem and ask God for direction. As you shift your focus, you will alter your life.

Reflection

_____

_____

_____

_____

_____

_____

_____

_____

_____

_____

_____

_____

_____

_____

Action

_____

_____

_____

_____

_____

_____

_____

_____

_____

_____

_____

_____

_____

Day 77: THE CONSUMING FIRE

What does it take to ignite a fire? A match is extremely small, but it is often the beginning cause of a great flame. Once that fire gets going, it will continue to burn, and it will only get stronger as you add wood or any other flammable substance.

No matter how small you may feel your gift or purpose is, it can grow into an all-consuming fire. Once you allow God to use your gifts for his purpose, there will be a burning fire on the inside of you that cannot be blown out. Occasionally, some individuals may attempt to throw some water on it and cool you off, but, once that flame gets hot enough, nothing will be able to stop you. If you put an item close to a burning fire, the flames will consume the object. In the same way, as you continue to use your gifts, your fire will continuously burn, and others will be touched by your abilities and testimony.

Reflection

_____
_____
_____
_____
_____
_____
_____
_____
_____
_____
_____
_____
_____

Action

_____
_____
_____
_____
_____
_____
_____
_____
_____
_____
_____
_____
_____

Day 78: FINANCIAL FUTURE

Are you satisfied with your money management skills? I encourage you to take the time now to develop basic skills and protect your credit history. The reason I am addressing this subject is because, every day, I meet too many people who are struggling financially because of poor decisions that were made at a young age. One way to avoid financial disasters is to develop good habits now. A key area of concern is not so much how much you make but how much you spend. Of course, we all like to look nice, but the key to building a solid future is to have balance. Take ten minutes out of your busy schedule and examine where you currently stand financially. I want you to succeed in all areas of life. Similar to how we all have reputations within our social lives, your credit score is your financial reputation. Set those financial goals and push yourself past ordinary limits.

LIVE IT

Reflection

_____
_____
_____
_____
_____
_____
_____
_____
_____
_____
_____
_____
_____
_____
_____
_____

Action

_____
_____
_____
_____
_____
_____
_____
_____
_____
_____
_____
_____
_____
_____
_____
_____

Day 79: IT'S ON YOU

We often find ourselves in compromising positions or in situations that we no longer desire to be a part of our lives. If you know you are connected to someone who has direct intentions to ruin your life, then it's your job to say "no more." It's your job to say, "It's gone too far, and I'm not going one more step forward in this direction." Too many times, we have heard people say they know a certain person is not good for them, but they are allowing this certain person to still be a part of their lives. Well, it's on you to get out. It is on you to decide that your future is way too important to remain in a dreadful situation. If you are allowing someone negative to occupy your time, you are limiting your potential. If this is the only life that you will ever live, why should you allow someone else to dictate your actions? You are the only boss of your life, and no one has authority over it but God. God is the only one with a flawless track record. You do have a choice, so you do not have to take what someone else is handing you in life. Be authentic to you.

LIVE IT

Reflection

_____
_____
_____
_____
_____
_____
_____
_____
_____
_____
_____
_____
_____
_____

Action

_____
_____
_____
_____
_____
_____
_____
_____
_____
_____
_____
_____
_____
_____

Day 80: SUCCESS OVER FAILURE

Simply put, there is entirely too much failure and disappointment in the world today. Too many people seem to be more concerned with what they do not have and what they are not able to accomplish. If you look back over your life, I think you will definitely find some victories. If you are so focused on what you feel you do not have, how will you remain confident in your future?

What if I were to ask you what you will accomplish over the next one, five, ten, and twenty years? Of course, we live life one day at a time, but you need a plan of action, a strategy, faith, and true desire. If you watch the news or listen to the radio, you will hear many stories of failure. There are too many available opportunities today for young people who are willing to make it happen. In order to take advantage of those opportunities, you must prepare now. It would be a shame for the chance you have been dreaming of to pass you by because you were not prepared. Remember, you only fail when you quit, and everything may not always go your way. You will have your ups and downs, but both are opportunities to gain great wisdom.

Reflection

_____
_____
_____
_____
_____
_____
_____
_____
_____
_____
_____
_____
_____
_____

Action

_____
_____
_____
_____
_____
_____
_____
_____
_____
_____
_____
_____
_____
_____

Day 81: ACTIVATE THE GIFT

Which is worse: 1) When you do not know what you are supposed to be doing, or 2) When you know what you should be doing, but you still do not do it? A cell phone with no signal does you no good. A car with no gas will not get you anywhere. Knowledge does not equal power, but the "use of knowledge is power." It does me no good to read a book two or three times and never apply what I have learned to my everyday life. The documents on a computer are of no use to you if you do not have the power cord that plugs into the wall and gives you a source of power.

It works the same way in our lives. You need a source of power that you can plug into and activate your gift. Make that dream a reality and stop wishing you had the gifts of another individual. If other people have achieved success in their chosen fields, be happy for them. Choose your path and take action immediately while using your gift to be a blessing to others. No one can beat you at being you. Activate the gift.

Reflection

_____

_____

_____

_____

_____

_____

_____

_____

_____

_____

_____

_____

_____

_____

_____

Action

_____

_____

_____

_____

_____

_____

_____

_____

_____

_____

_____

_____

_____

_____

_____

Day 82: I DARE YOU NOT TO QUIT

Think about how many times you have chosen to give up on something. Analyze the choices you have made so far in your life and decide whether you are traveling a path that is leading toward your dream life. If you are not passionate about what you wake up and do every morning, then you are more likely to quit.

Listen closely to the next statement. No matter where you are now, your next moves determine whether you remain stagnant or begin pursuing a life that utilizes your natural, God-given gifts. You cannot afford to quit. You are the CEO of your own life, and your time is extremely valuable. Laziness, procrastination, and lack of action are diseases of the mind that limit your desired future. Quitting is so easy because it does not require you to think. That is why we need to remove the phrase "I can't" from our vocabularies because it limits our ability to think past ordinary results. Do not accept words of discouragement from negative individuals. Turn those negative words into motivational thoughts that push you to achieve results that are beyond anything anyone in your family has ever dreamed of. Since you are the CEO, you do the hiring and firing while making the decisions about what stays and what gets removed from your life.

Reflection

_____
_____
_____
_____
_____
_____
_____
_____
_____
_____
_____
_____
_____
_____
_____

Action

_____
_____
_____
_____
_____
_____
_____
_____
_____
_____
_____
_____
_____
_____
_____

Day 83: PAIN IS AN INDICATOR...

When a woman is about to have a baby, she experiences great pain. The closer the time comes for the birth of the baby, the greater the pain gets. Then, she has the baby, and the pain is overcome by the beautiful birth of her child. Our lives work the same way. The closer you get to your purpose and end goal, the greater the pain gets, so stick to your plan and have patience because the pain will increase as you get closer to the goal that is about to be birthed into existence. Quitting is not in a great man's or woman's vocabulary.

When was the last time you did something knowing that it was outside of your comfort zone? Maybe it was something physical like implementing a stretching or exercise routine. Yes, it probably felt a bit painful as the stretch was taking place. However, it is important to note that the stretching extends your reach, literally and figuratively. This current stretch is happening for a reason that goes far beyond your personal understanding.

Reflection

_____
_____
_____
_____
_____
_____
_____
_____
_____
_____
_____
_____
_____
_____

Action

_____
_____
_____
_____
_____
_____
_____
_____
_____
_____
_____
_____
_____
_____
_____
_____

Day 84: YOU ARE THE ARTIST, SO PAINT YOUR PORTRAIT

The paintbrush is in your hands. The rest of your life is like a blank canvas. Remember that, when the final stroke is made on your self-portrait, you have to sign your name at the bottom of what you have created. You get to choose whether you create a priceless masterpiece or a mess of colors on a white piece of paper. Are you going to give someone else control of your paintbrush and allow them to paint your life to their liking?

Some of us have been letting our friends and people in the world push us around for far too long. Time does not stop for anyone. Basically, you are allowing precious time to pass you by because you are too afraid of what others may think of you if they find out how smart you really are, as well as what you are capable of accomplishing. You may lose some friends, and you may gain some new ones, but at the end of the day, you must be satisfied with your own decisions. Decide today to be a true artist and paint your portrait as you see fit. There will never be anyone from the past, present, or future that will have your uniqueness, so go make history.

Reflection

_____
_____
_____
_____
_____
_____
_____
_____
_____
_____
_____
_____
_____
_____

Action

_____
_____
_____
_____
_____
_____
_____
_____
_____
_____
_____
_____
_____
_____
_____

Day 85: PUSH BACK

At some point in our lives, we have all faced a situation where we felt defeated and unsure of tomorrow. You were so caught up in that situation that you lost focus and felt mentally, emotionally, and physically drained. It is only natural. It is okay to cry when you have been hurt or be angry about an unfavorable situation. However, you cannot allow yourself to stay in that unstable condition.

The same way you get up to go to school or work every morning is the same way opposition goes to work in your life. Opposition often comes in familiar cycles presenting the same old tricks time and again. Same cycle, different people. Opposition is pushing for control and putting pressure on your mind by bringing up the past. The cycles of opposition remind you of previous mistakes, taking authority over your thoughts. The reason for this is to prevent you from moving forward and fulfilling your purpose. You desire peace and a comfortable lifestyle, and opposition presents confusion and poverty, sometimes literally and physically. Opposition will push until you feel defeated. It's time to PUSH BACK!

Reflection

_____
_____
_____
_____
_____
_____
_____
_____
_____
_____
_____
_____
_____
_____
_____
_____

Action

_____
_____
_____
_____
_____
_____
_____
_____
_____
_____
_____
_____
_____
_____
_____
_____

Day 86: I'VE FALLEN, AND I MUST GET UP (Part 3)

Now that you have identified your enemy, you can overcome. However, do not necessarily expect your world to change overnight. We must go through a process in order to work our way out of a bad situation. At the same time, we need to commit ourselves to a changed lifestyle so that we do not fall for the same tricks over and over again. This often requires us to separate ourselves from certain friendships. If you are still connected to the same people who played a role in keeping you down, how are you going to change? You need to get connected to some people that are going in a direction filled with purpose.

Someone once told me, "Look at the habits and characteristics of the five people you spend the majority of your time with because it is a great indicator of where you will be in five years." So watch who you listen to and take the time to look deeper into the situation yourself before automatically accepting the opinions of others. Your friends may laugh or get angry at the new you, but it's okay because some people are only meant to be in your life for a season. Again, You Must Get Up! Make the decision today that you will not remain stuck in your uncomfortable condition. Release the disappointments of yesterday. Decide today that you are tired of standing in quicksand. Decide that you are ready to build a solid foundation.

Reflection

_____

_____

_____

_____

_____

_____

_____

_____

_____

_____

_____

_____

_____

_____

_____

_____

Action

_____

_____

_____

_____

_____

_____

_____

_____

_____

_____

_____

_____

_____

_____

Day 87: MEDIOCRITY STOPS HERE

Do you have room for mediocrity in your life? I certainly do not. Anyone can be average and live a mediocre life. It does not require you to think, and it requires no self-discipline. Anyone can follow the crowd and allow the world to push them around. It has become evident to me that, if you are not convinced and fully persuaded that God has something greater for your life, then you will be average.

There is not a person alive that can force you to change. You have to make the decision that you are "sick and tired of being sick and tired." The desire to change must be greater than the pain you are enduring in your current state of mind. So, if you are not happy with your current situation, only you have the power to say, "I've had enough, and mediocrity stops here." All the great men and women that I have met have these characteristics in common: self-discipline, perseverance, desire, right mental attitude, confidence, and the passion to exceed an ordinary agenda on the way to greatness. Mediocrity stops here.

Reflection

_____
_____
_____
_____
_____
_____
_____
_____
_____
_____
_____
_____
_____
_____

Action

_____
_____
_____
_____
_____
_____
_____
_____
_____
_____
_____
_____
_____

Day 88: INVEST IN YOURSELF (Pt. 3)

We've already discussed how to invest in yourself in parts 1 and 2, so let's deal with the final area. The final part is using your natural, God-given gifts to be an example for others.

Once you've established an understanding of who you are and where you're going, it is important to think beyond yourself. It's time to invest in others. The seeds that you plant should produce harvests long after you are gone.

What's keeping you from sharing your greatness with others?

Go teach a class. Volunteer somewhere. Daily ask yourself, who am I bringing with me? If the answer is no one, it's time to reevaluate and reinvest to get a better return.

Make a list of activities you can do or be a part of. Identify a few people that could benefit from your knowledge. As you are being poured into, take the time to pour into someone else. This is much bigger than you.

Do not look down when you walk and walk with strides of boldness, courage, and confidence. And take someone else with you. Investments grow in increments over time.

LIVE IT

Reflection

_____
_____
_____
_____
_____
_____
_____
_____
_____
_____
_____
_____
_____
_____

Action

_____
_____
_____
_____
_____
_____
_____
_____
_____
_____
_____
_____
_____
_____
_____

Day 89: MAINTAIN THE ENTHUSIASM

After investing in yourself, it is crucially important to maintain your enthusiasm. Throughout the course of the week, you may run into a variety of distractions that are designed to get you off-course.

Have you ever been very excited about something in the beginning stages, but over time, that excitement fades away? The best way to maintain that passion is to stir up the gift. The key is to remain focused on the goals you have set for yourself and constantly remind yourself of what you are attempting to achieve. You face the risk of losing interest when you do not constantly stir up the gift you possess. Write down what you want to achieve so you have a visual reminder of what you are working toward. If you feel yourself drifting away or losing interest, just go back to the initial notes.

Yes, it is hard work, but it will keep you on course so that you remain focused. Anyone can give up, quit, or start something new every two weeks. However, it takes true character and integrity to remain committed and follow through on the promises that, most importantly, you have made to yourself.

Reflection

_____
_____
_____
_____
_____
_____
_____
_____
_____
_____
_____
_____
_____
_____
_____
_____

Action

_____
_____
_____
_____
_____
_____
_____
_____
_____
_____
_____
_____
_____
_____
_____
_____

Day 90: HOW DOES IT FEEL TO HAVE YOUR MASTER'S DEGREE?

I commend you for making it thus far in your life. How does it feel to be so young and already have been presented with your master's degree? This is not the type of degree that you receive from an educational institution. You only receive this degree by recognizing and walking with the heavenly authority in your life. This has been awarded to you because you are connected to the creator of all degrees.

I have often heard the statement, "To whom much is given, much is required." With your newly achieved status and because you now know you have this prestigious certification, it is time to fulfill your purpose. Over the past few months, you may have felt unqualified or as if you have lacked certain qualities. Well, yesterday was the last day that lack paid you a visit. Rather than looking down, look up, and acknowledge the master who is reaching down to hand you your degree. Will you accept this honor?

Reflection

Action

KEEP MOVING

So you have made it to the end of this inspirational journey. Congratulations!! I hope that this will be more than the ending of a book, but rather the beginning of a new you. The great part about it is that we have designed it so that you can reread and share the content without it being overwhelming. In the days ahead, go back and look at what you wrote in the notes section. It is an absolutely great way to measure your growth, and it is quite possible that you'll have a few "aha" moments. Be sure to share the impact of this content with others that you know so that they too can be inspired toward greater. Thank you again for picking up this book. I trust that it will have a lasting impact.

LIVE IT

Reflection

_____
_____
_____
_____
_____
_____
_____
_____
_____
_____
_____
_____
_____
_____
_____

Action

_____
_____
_____
_____
_____
_____
_____
_____
_____
_____
_____
_____
_____
_____

BONUS

Bonus Day 1: IS A U-TURN PERMITTED?

Do you need to make a U-turn? If you honestly ask yourself this question, your inner voice will give you the right answer. You can either choose to pretend like you do not know the truth and lie to yourself, or you can decide that it's time for a U-turn. You may need to make a U-turn ASAP because the world is leading you in the direction that it desires for you to go. The world does not control you. If you continue on the same beaten path, you will wake up many years from now seriously unhappy. The path you are following today is bigger than you.

Our decisions today determine how we will live years from now. It is certainly okay to enjoy life, but we have to use wisdom. You do not want to get so far out there that, when you turn around, you do not recognize how you got to this place in your life. Next time you are driving down the road and you pass that U-turn sign, ask yourself if you need to make a turnaround in your life. Again, we are all imperfect, but we don't have to stay in a dead situation. Things can get back on track, regardless of the number of wrong turns. Sometimes, we need to see what did not work in order to appreciate the success ahead.

Reflection

_____
_____
_____
_____
_____
_____
_____
_____
_____
_____
_____
_____
_____

Action

_____
_____
_____
_____
_____
_____
_____
_____
_____
_____
_____
_____
_____
_____

Bonus Day 2: DO NOT BE DECEIVED

What has drawn your attention away from the truth and enticed your mind? Oftentimes, we get so caught up in what initially appeals to our eyes that we do not take the time to carefully weigh the rewards versus the risks. You are too rare and carefully fashioned by God to fall prey to the disguised plans of your greatest predator. The enemy is the master of deception, and he desires to see you fall and continuously drift away from your destination. He will consistently attempt to trick you with false appearances that are intended to keep you from seeing the truth.

God has already planted purpose and victory into your journey if only you will keep your eyes focused on his will for your life. We need to have discernment in our daily walks throughout life because, in today's times, it is too easy to fall into dark situations. The enemy is after your mind so that he can control your daily actions while capturing your heart and destroying your soul. First glances can be dangerous, so take the time to analyze the long-term consequences of temporary fulfillments.

BONUS

Reflection

_____
_____
_____
_____
_____
_____
_____
_____
_____
_____
_____
_____
_____
_____

Action

_____
_____
_____
_____
_____
_____
_____
_____
_____
_____
_____
_____
_____
_____

Bonus Day 3: THE ENEMY WANTS SOME RECOGNITION

Everyone likes to be rewarded for his or her work. Whether it is at work, school, or home, we all like to be recognized for our hard work. At the same time, there is an enemy after that same recognition.

When the devil tries to attack us and we resist his deceitful tricks, he does not get recognition. He is putting in a lot of hard work to get recognition in our lives, but we must choose to be more than conquerors. He wants to live in our hearts and destroy our plans for success. We must begin to think, act, and speak like we are already in our positions of success.

Even if you are not initially recognized, continue to work diligently. In due time, you will see the results of all the hard work, perseverance, and determination that you have already sown.

Reflection

_____
_____
_____
_____
_____
_____
_____
_____
_____
_____
_____
_____
_____
_____

Action

_____
_____
_____
_____
_____
_____
_____
_____
_____
_____
_____
_____
_____
_____

Bonus Day 4: TIME'S UP

Once we get sick and tired of being in an unfulfilling or boring situation, we become very anxious to do other activities. We begin to check our watches, and we cannot wait until the hour comes when we can leave that boring event, long class, or intense day at work.

The same goes for the enemy in your life. His time is up because we are claiming victory in every area of your life on this day. No longer will he be allowed to constantly bring the past into the forefront of your mind. He wants to remind you of the mistakes you have made in the past so that he can hinder you from fulfilling your destiny, but Time's Up. If you are willing to walk with faith and know that God is the only authority, then the enemy must leave your life. Everyone deals with different situations, so it is crucially important that we do not feel isolated from one another. You need some people in your corner that can encourage you, and you must understand that you are not the only person to ever go through what you are currently facing. Next time you check your watch or cell phone for the time, remember that the enemy's time is up as well.

BONUS

Reflection

_____
_____
_____
_____
_____
_____
_____
_____
_____
_____
_____
_____
_____

Action

_____
_____
_____
_____
_____
_____
_____
_____
_____
_____
_____
_____
_____

Bonus Day 5: ALL EYES ON YOU

What we do in the dark will eventually come into the light. Whether you notice it or not, someone is always watching. When you are moving closer to your goals, people tend to watch your every move. A few may want to see you succeed, but many are just waiting for you to make a mistake.

What does that mean to you? It means you have to be mindful of who you surround yourself with each and every day. As we overcome difficult trials and defeat the enemy's attacks, we grow stronger in wisdom. By surrounding yourself with wise people, you can avoid a lot of the mistakes that have previously been made by others. Since all eyes are on you, give them something to watch. Set the example by living with integrity, having faith, and maximizing your potential.

Reflection

_____

_____

_____

_____

_____

_____

_____

_____

_____

_____

_____

_____

_____

_____

_____

Action

_____

_____

_____

_____

_____

_____

_____

_____

_____

_____

_____

_____

_____

_____

ABOUT THE AUTHOR

Alex L. Brown is a speaker, community leader, pastor, entrepreneur, and now an author. What simply began as a dream for an eight-year-old kid has now grown into a commitment to impacting lives. Over the last decade, he has invested time speaking and serving as a unique voice across the nation. Alex's story is one that resonates with many as he often shares what he and his family have overcome and continue to pursue. His early childhood days included being raised in a military household and then being parented by a single mother with three other siblings.

He is a husband and father to an incredible family that currently resides in metro Atlanta. Today he continues to author inspirational writings, speak, and travel, while using his God-given gifts to impact thousands.

Alex's passion to see others overcome life challenges, move on from the past, achieve their dreams, and fulfill their purpose inspired him to create ABrown Enterprises.

His first book, *Think It. Be It.* Live It. is more than mere words. It is evidence of what happens when you do not give up and are inspired to see others achieve greater.

ACKNOWLEDGEMENTS

I want to thank my siblings Arthur, Joshua, and Stacy for your continuous support during this writing process. Thank you to my father Dr. Arthur Brown II and spiritual advisor Dr. Marquis Boone for your advice and support. Thank you to our editor and partner E. Danielle Butler. You have made this process incredibly smooth and were so timely with your communication. Special thanks to my friend and assistant Natalie for putting up with me daily. Thank you to every friend who chooses to be a supportive voice. You know who you are. Thank you to my mother-in-love Rubbie Blasingame for being a mother to me as well, and for being a consistent place in my life.

Lastly, I have to acknowledge my mother. Long before anyone knew me, you saw something in me that encouraged me to live beyond the darkest days of my life. I made you a promise as a kid and I'm committed to it for the rest of my life. Again, thank you all for being so encouraging. My life is better because you share yours with me.

ABROWN ENTERPRISES

Other Brands:

B Candid Clothing
https://www.bcandidco.com/

Connect:

@alex_lbrown
(Instagram, Twitter)

If this book was useful to you, why not share it with your family, friends, leaders, and mentees? Take a moment to leave a review on Amazon and my website so that others can:
Think It. Be It. Live It.!

Made in the USA
Columbia, SC
16 October 2020

22982122R00131